FROM VIENNA TO VERSAILLES

From Vienna to Versailles

by

L. C. B. SEAMAN

METHUEN & CO LTD

11 NEW FETTER LANE · EC4

First published July 28, 1955
Reprinted 1960
Reprinted in this size 1964, 1965, 1967 *and* 1969
ISBN 0 423 70820 1

First published as a University Paperback 1964
Reprinted four times
Reprinted 1970
Reprinted 1972
Reprinted 1975 *and* 1976
ISBN 0 416 68330 4

Printed in Great Britain by
Whitstable Litho Ltd., Whitstable, Kent

Distributed in the USA by
HARPER AND ROW, PUBLISHERS INC.
BARNES AND NOBLE IMPORT DIVISION

CONTENTS

MAPS

PREFACE

THE aim of this book is not to re-tell but to re-examine the story of European affairs from 1815 to 1920, chiefly, though not exclusively, from the point of view of international relations. Designed chiefly as a work of elucidation and interpretation, it is addressed mainly to those who already have some acquaintance with the main events and personalities of the period. The justification for producing such a book is that it is badly needed. No period of European history is more widely studied than that covered by this book; yet few periods seem to be more widely misunderstood, or more obscured by the perpetuation of generalizations that belong more properly to the status of legend.

Among the legends that mislead the student of nineteenth century history are, for example, the idea that there was such a thing as a 'congress system'; that middle class discontent caused the 1848 revolutions; that Napoleon III 'overthrew' the Second Republic; that the Crimean War was caused by the decline of the Turkish Empire; that Bismarck unified Germany and that Cavour wanted to unify Italy; that Bismarck secured Russian neutrality by his Polish policy in 1863, that he deceived Napoleon III at Biarritz, and that he regained Russian friendship by the Reinsurance Treaty; that the Anglo-Japanese Alliance of 1902 ended Britain's splendid isolation; that a condition of international anarchy existed in the decade before 1914; and that the 1919 settlement weakened central and eastern Europe by 'balkanizing' it.

Most of these statements are inaccurate; and though the writer naturally makes no claim to be the first to realize this, he does suggest that this is the first attempt within the covers of one conveniently-sized work to explain why they are inaccurate.

In its approach to the problems dealt with the book sets out to be provocative and emphatic. This is deliberate, and the writer does not feel it necessary to apologize if in some places he may appear somewhat dogmatic. The writing of history, and the study of it, have suffered much from what Sidney Smith accused Bishops of looking for in young curates—'a certain dropping-down-deadness of manner'. Historical study that does not challenge the reader to think hard is poor stuff. Our universities continue to complain that the schools send them too many students who regard history solely as a matter of acquiring information. They are right to complain if this is in fact true; but after vainly searching for twenty years for an authoritative one-volume book on the nineteenth century that provided students with an example of how to interpret facts as well as how to recite them in chronological order, the writer is inclined to direct the charge back upon those from whom it issues. He has written this book solely because those best qualified to produce such a work have so far failed to do so.

There is only a very short bibliography. There seems no point in encumbering these pages with yet one more list of the inevitable authorities. The writer does feel it necessary, however, to append a list of the works which might be described as the formative influences behind the treatment of some of the main topics dealt with in this volume. In mentioning these works, the writer hastens to disclaim all intention of saddling their distinguished authors with any responsibility whatever for any of the judgments contained herein.

L.C.B.S.

BIBLIOGRAPHY

The Congress of Vienna	Sir Harold Nicolson
The Aftermath of the Napoleonic Wars	H. G. Schenk
The Foreign Policy of Palmerston, 1830–1841	Sir Charles Webster
Le Coup du Deux Décembre	Henri Guillemin
The Course of German History	A. J. P. Taylor
The Habsburg Monarchy	A. J. P. Taylor
Bismarck and the German Empire	E. Eyck
Cavour and Garibaldi, 1860	D. Mack Smith
European Alliances and Alignments	W. L. Langer
Studies in Diplomacy	G. P. Gooch
Twenty-Five Years	Viscount Grey of Fallodon
Grey of Fallodon	G. M. Trevelyan
History of 'The Times' (*Vol. III*: 1884–1912)	
Brest-Litovsk: The Forgotten Peace	J. W. Wheeler-Bennett

This book was in a very advanced stage of preparation before the appearance of Mr A. J. P. Taylor's volume *The Struggle for Mastery in Europe*, 1848–1918. Some account of Mr Taylor's views in that work was taken into consideration in the final revision of the latter part of Chapter XIII and the early part of Chapter XV. In general, however, the writer considers himself fortunate to have written this book while Mr Taylor's work was still unavailable. He is thereby absolved from the accusation of being either Mr Taylor's echo, which would perhaps be too easy, or his competitor, which would be both difficult and presumptuous.

SUPPLEMENTARY BIBLIOGRAPHY

The following is a short list of works which had not been published when this book was first written and which deal more closely with some of the issues it raises or set them within their wider context.

Prelude to Modern Europe, 1815–1914, Sir Llewellyn Woodward, 1972. Published shortly after the author's death, this is an ideal short book to be studied in conjunction with *From Vienna to Versailles* since it displays wisdom and scholarship on many different aspects of European history in the period indicated.

Post-Victorian Britain, 1902–51, L. C. B. Seaman, 1966, contains, in chapter 5, a somewhat less favourable view of Sir Edward Grey than is found herein and, in chapter 12, a closer examination of the problems of peace-making in Europe after 1918.

Europe in the Nineteenth Century, H. Hearder, 1965, is a cool and temperate study of European history to 1880.

The Concert of Europe, 1815–1914, René Albrecht-Carrié, 1968, has a valuable collection of documents.

Italy, a modern history, D. Mack Smith, 1959, should be read in conjunction with the same author's *The Making of Italy*, 1796–1870, published 1968, which is largely documentary.

Germany 1789–1919, Agatha Ramm, 1967, and *The Mind of Germany*, Hans Kohn, 1961, are both valuable studies.

The Political System of Napoleon III, T. Zeldin, 1958, greatly illuminates the methods by which the Second Empire was maintained internally.

The Franco–Prussian War, Michael Howard, 1962, is a comprehensive and balanced examination of the conduct of the war on both sides.

The Habsburg Monarchy, 1790–1918, C. A. Macartney, 1968, is a large book, concentrating mainly on the period before 1867, but the best available on the subject.

The Foreign Policy of Victorian England, K. Bourne, 1970, is a somewhat breathless summary, supplementing a useful collection of documents.

The Reluctant Imperialists, C. J. Lowe, Vols I & II, 1967, analyses British foreign policy 1878–1902, volume II being a collection of documents.

The End of Isolation, G. Monger, 1963, is a study of British foreign policy in the decisive years 1900–1907 and is indispensable for this period.

Land and Power: British and Allied Policy on Germany's Frontiers, 1916–19, H. I. Nelson, 1963, casts much light on how the territorial settlement of 1919 was finally achieved.

I

THE VIENNA SETTLEMENT

THE two extreme views about the makers of the 1815 settlement have both been expressed by Sir Harold Nicolson. One is that they were 'mere hucksters in the diplomatic market, bartering the happiness of millions with a scented smile'. This he denies. The opposite view, which he appears to accept, is that 'they did in fact prevent a general European conflagration for a whole century of time'. We may agree with his dismissal of the first of these views; but a study of what actually happened in the nineteenth century must make us almost as unwilling to accept the second view.

A dislike of the 1815 settlement was normal among historians for so long because it was held to have ignored the great principles of Liberalism and Nationalism. The essential rightness of these two principles was taken for granted. The history of the nineteenth century was regarded largely as the story of the slow, but inevitable and rightful, triumph of these two ideas over the principles of reaction which the 1815 settlement, it was claimed, sought to embody as the permanent basis of the European order. With the rigidly reactionary character of the 1815 settlement was contrasted the democratic and progressive spirit of the Versailles settlement of 1919. 'Earth's wormy dynasties re-robe,' wrote Hardy in *The Dynasts*, concerning the events of 1815. In 1919 those dynasties crumbled to dust, to be replaced by a world made 'safe for democracy' and devoted to 'the self-determination of peoples'. Woodrow Wilson had been a professor of history; and this may account for the lofty pronouncement that in the settlement he had in mind 'peoples and provinces' would not be 'bandied about like pawns in a game'. At all costs, it seemed in 1919, Europe must be spared another Congress of Vienna.

It is therefore necessary to consider carefully what the attitude of the statesmen of Vienna really was to the question of nationalism. One may recall Castlereagh's subsequent comment on the aims of the powers who had won the war and made the peace. 'It was an Union for the re-conquest of the greater part of the Continent of Europe from the military domination of France.' As a result of the labours of these men, French soldiers and administrators were expelled from the Netherlands, from Germany, Switzerland, Italy, Spain and Portugal. From all these areas there was removed the menace of conscription into the armies of a foreign despot, or the threat of having to fight in an army forcibly devoted to that despot's ambitions. Perhaps it is so rarely mentioned because it is so obvious; but there were far fewer people being ruled and despoiled by foreigners by the end of 1815 than there were at the end of 1810.

Neither is it an altogether valid criticism of Vienna to say that it was concerned solely with restoring the rights of royal and princely property owners and never with the rights of 'the peoples'. The formula of Legitimacy loomed much larger in the conversation of Talleyrand than in the clauses of the Treaty of Vienna. The notion that Vienna was solely concerned to restore legitimate rulers breaks down after only the briefest examination. It was ignored in Western Germany, in Poland, Saxony, Norway, the Austrian Netherlands and Northern Italy. It was most conspicuously applied to the French Bourbons; but it was almost exclusively in their interest that the slogan was invented.

It is true that 'peoples' were not liberated in the sense that Fichte and Stein appeared to want the Germans to be liberated, that is from the control of a motley of hereditary princelings.

EUROPE in 1815
DENMARK
Copenhagen
Konigsberg
Danzig
UNITED KINGDOM
Schleswig
HOLSTEIN
Hamburg
MECKLENBG
Bremen
HANOVER
Hanover
Berlin
Posen
Vistula
Bug
RUSSIA
London
KINGDOM OF THE NETHERLANDS
Warsaw
POLAND
(Congress Kingdom)
WESTPHALIA
Cologne
HESSE
Coblenz
Gotha
Weimar
SAXON STATES
SAXONY
Elbe
Oder
Breslau
Republic
Cracow
Lemberg
Dniester
BESSARABIA
Bayreuth
Paris
Metz
Strassburg
Heidelberg
Stuttgart
Munich
Vienna
Pressburg
Theiss
Pruth
MOLDAVIA
FRANCE
Berne
SWITZERLAND
Innsbruck
AUSTRIAN EMPIRE
HUNGARY
Budapest
Laibach
Trieste
Drave
Save
WALLACHIA
Bucharest
DOBRUJA
Milan
Venice
Turin
PIEDMONT
SAVOY
Parma
Rhône
Belgrade
Danube
Sistova
Varna
BOSNIA
SERVIA
BULGARIA
Nice
Genoa
S. MARINO
GRD D. OF TUSCANY
PAPAL STATES
OTTOMAN EMPIRE
Sofia
Adrianople
Constantinople
MONTENEGRO
CORSICA
(To France)
Rome
KINGDOM OF THE TWO SICILIES
Salonika
Naples
SARDINIA
Messina
Ionian Is. (Br.)
Athens
Patras
GREECE
Palermo
Catania
Prussia
Austrian Empire
Ottoman Empire
Kingdom of Sardinia
Boundary of the German Confederation

But acceptance of the principle of nationalism in this sense was, in the circumstances of 1815, either impossible, or undesirable, or both.

The Belgians, to take first the people who were to achieve their liberation from foreigners earlier than others, were transferred, without their consent, from the Habsburg Empire to the Kingdom of the Netherlands. But an independent Belgium would have been thought in 1815 to have no chance of survival at all, because of its perilous proximity to France. Not even all the Belgians wanted independence, even in 1830; and the solution arrived at, that of neutrality under a European guarantee, was achieved only because it was then clear—as it certainly was not in 1815—that France, under Louis Philippe, was manageable, and because Palmerston could devote to the working out of the solution an amount of time and patience quite impossible for Castlereagh or anybody else in the crowded months of 1815. With the experience of the Hundred Days in their minds, the men of Vienna would have considered it a betrayal both of the general peace and of the Belgians to give them an 'independence' that would have left them defenceless in the path of the largest and most aggressive nation in western Europe.

Nor can the failure of the Kingdom of the Netherlands be ascribed to the 1815 arrangements. This was due to the failure of the House of Orange to apply faithfully the spirit and the terms of the document on which the union of the two regions was based. The men of 1815 imposed on the Dutch the duty of guaranteeing religious toleration and commercial equality to their new Belgian subjects. So that not even the Belgians were bandied about like pawns in a game in 1815. If anybody committed that mistake, it was the Dutch between 1815 and 1830.

In Germany, it is difficult to see how the peacemakers could have settled in 1815 a problem which over fifty years later was solved (and even so 'solved' is much too strong a word) only by the disastrous methods of Bismarck. The unification of Germany was not in the realm of practical politics in 1815. Nobody represented at the Congress wanted it. Prussia and Austria, two of the five chief powers, abhorred the notion, and remembering how strenuously Talleyrand resisted the aggrandisement of Prussia, one can imagine how much more he would have resisted the creation of a united Germany. Statesmen can only be criticized for failing to do what is possible. Diplomats cannot be criticized for not wanting to negotiate their countries out of existence; and the creation of a unitary Germany would have involved the representatives of Austria and Prussia in doing precisely that.

It is doubtless arguable that what was possible in 1815 was a German Confederation less carefully designed to be powerless, and less devoid of meaning to the Germans. Yet, if the chief German protest in the years after 1815 was against the pettiness of *Kleinstaaterei*, it is worth remembering that the 1815 settlement did in fact ensure that the number of states in the Bund was smaller by hundreds than the number that had existed in the Holy Roman Empire. The Germany of 1815 was, since Vienna did not undo the work of Napoleon in western Germany, much less divided than it had been in 1789. Nor must it be forgotten, as it so frequently is, that the act setting up the Confederation required the rulers of the German states to establish constitutions. Although the Carlsbad Decrees were designed to nullify this provision, liberal constitutions of a sort were not banished from Germany in the years after Vienna either in theory or in practice; and their absence was in any case not prescribed by the 1815 settlement.

The settlement of Italy may seem the most objectionable part of the arrangements in western Europe. Save in the Kingdom of Sardinia, and with the doubtful exception of the Papal States, Italy was given over more completely than ever to the rule of the foreigner, owing to the fact that in Italy as in western Germany, the Vienna settlement compounded with Napoleonic felony—the Venetian Republic was not restored, and passed into the hands of the Habsburgs. Yet how criminal was it to place northern Italy in Habsburg hands in 1815? It was in the Italian campaign that Bonapartism was born. It was to be in Italy that Napoleon III would conduct his only successful war of aggression in Europe. The lesson of the past was that the abdication of Austrian control in Italy was likely to result, not in Italian freedom, but in Italian subjection to France. Moreover, time was to prove that the problem of the Papal States, to name no other, was susceptible only of a military solution. In 1815, after twenty years of war, the aim was quite properly to do only such things as could be achieved by diplomacy in the interests of general peace. It is possible to argue that united Italy was brought to birth prematurely in 1870; there is all the more to be said for not expecting it to arise from the deliberations of 1815. What may reasonably be criticized is Metternich's refusal to see that the Napoleonic period had made differences in Italy which time and diplomacy could not of themselves eradicate. Metternich's fault was that he relied too simply on the therapeutic value of diplomacy. Diplomacy—or rather his particular type of diplomacy—could, he thought, keep the Great Powers in agreement. War would thus be avoided. In the maintenance of a long period of calm and repose lay the only chance that the peoples might settle down quietly and that the noisy clamour of 'intellectuals' and romantics in Italy, as in Germany, might be suffocated by the universal torpor. The fault of the Vienna statesmen is not that they put the clock back in 1815 (at least they did so only in the sense that Napoleon might be said to have caused it to move too fast); their error was that they hoped to keep the clock stopped at 1815 for the next half-century. This was certainly the aim of Metternich, the Russians and the Prussians; and their negative policy in the years after 1815 is far more at fault than the treaty itself.

The plight of Poland was to occupy the thoughts and stimulate the self-righteousness of many English and French liberals all through the century. Yet that the problem of Poland occupied any time at all in 1815 was due solely to the equivocal desire of Alexander of Russia simultaneously to liberate Poland to satisfy his conscience, and to keep it to satisfy his Romanov pride. One might well apply to Alexander and his Polish plan the remark once made about Lord John Russell—'he always has such excellent motives for doing himself a good turn'.

The problem of Poland in 1815 raised in its crudest form the essential problem concerning a small nation state, namely that such a state is hardly ever truly independent. The disguise was exceptionally thin in the case of Alexander's proposed Kingdom of Poland. The enlargement of its area, chiefly, if indirectly, at the expense of the King of Saxony, to include Polish territory formerly under Prussia, together with the grant of a constitution—these apparent concessions to Polish national feeling deceived nobody but their author. What Alexander was trying to create was a Polish client-state by means of which he would extend Russian influence farther into Europe than ever before. His appeal to Polish patriotism was even more fraudulent than the similar appeal made by Alexander II in 1878 to the patriotism of the Bulgars. The rejection of his scheme by the other powers was both inevitable and statesmanlike. It frightened Metternich because it would extend Russian influence, and Talleyrand because it was tied up with the aggrandisement of Prussia at the expense of Saxony. The Poles lost nothing by this opposition. Freedom offered as an act of grace by a Romanov with a guilt-complex was meaningless, as subsequent events proved.

A final point is the transfer of Norway from Denmark to

Sweden. It is usually implied that this means that the Norwegians were integrated into Sweden regardless of their own wishes in the matter. This was certainly the original intention, but the Norwegians protested that such a procedure, if undertaken against the will of the inhabitants, was contrary to international law. They won their point. The Act of Union between the two countries declared that their unity had been achieved 'not by force of arms but by free conviction'; and Norway had its own government, parliament, army and navy. The great powers accepted this solution and since Norway had not been a separate kingdom since 1397, once more the men of 1815 can be defended against the charge of cynical indifference. The fact that the settlement of Norway endured till 1905 and was then ended peaceably, is sufficient indication that the difficulties that persisted through the century were not major ones.

Nevertheless the Vienna settlement must not be regarded as having of itself prevented European war for a century. It is possible to say instead that it contained in none of its provisions the seeds of a future war between the great powers, and must thus be rated a better peace than either Utrecht or Versailles. Utrecht rankled in the hearts of the Habsburgs: and its colonial and commercial clauses were an encouragement to the British to embark in due course on new wars against France and Spain. Versailles humiliated, or appeared to humiliate, the Germans; created new democratic states whose democracy had no roots and whose independent sovereignty was illusory; abolished old minority problems only to create new ones; disappointed the Italians and inflated the French; and by appealing to the irrational forces of the mass mind bred a chaos contrasting tragically with the orderliness that Vienna achieved by ignoring the masses altogether. For the disregard of Liberalism and Nationalism at Vienna (in so far as they were disregarded) did not cause war. They were right in thinking in 1815 that before revolutions can make wars, there must first be the wars that encourage the revolutions. They saw that the issues of peace and war are decided by the great powers and by them alone. Hence the simple fact that the Vienna settlement contained no clause that offered any of the great powers a pretext for war is its complete and sufficient justification.

Yet ultimately, wars are neither caused nor prevented by treaties, but by policies. What prevented a major war until 1853 was the determination of the great powers that there should not be such a war: a determination made easier by the fact that the Vienna settlement involved no major injustice to any one of them, not even to the defeated. The cause of peace was not seriously jeopardized until Louis Napoleon became Napoleon III. He was the first ruler of a great power consciously to desire the overthrow of the Vienna system: and it is his arrival on the scene that very largely accounts for the wars of the 1850's and 1860's. These wars broke the alliance of the great powers, on which the maintenance of the Vienna system depended, and then destroyed the Vienna settlement in Italy and Germany. By 1871 neither the territorial boundaries nor the political institutions of the European powers bore much resemblance to those of 1815. If there was peace in Europe for forty years after 1815, the credit must go mainly to Metternich, but also to Palmerston and to Nicholas I. That there were wars between 1853 and 1871 was due mainly to Napoleon III. That there was no general war between 1871 and 1914 does not mean that peace prevailed in any sense in that period. There might have been war in 1875, 1878, 1885, 1887, 1898, 1906, 1908, 1911 or 1912. That it was avoided on each of these occasions has nothing to do with the Congress of Vienna.

II

THE CONGRESS SYSTEM AND THE HOLY ALLIANCE 1815–1820

PERHAPS the most useful service a student can do himself in attempting to study great power co-operation in the years immediately after the Napoleonic Wars is to dismiss from his mind altogether the notion that there ever was such a thing as a Congress System. He may then have some chance of realizing that although there were Congresses after 1815 there was little that was systematic about them. There was no agreement between the powers as to what Congresses were for, and there was no permanent organization for international co-operation such as was set up after each of the two German wars of the twentieth century. Like so many of the 'systems' in history, the Congress System is an invention of historians.

The basis of the experiment in great power co-operation after 1815 was the conviction among the victors that, having won the war by their co-operation, only by continuing such co-operation could they hope to keep the peace. Since, also, the Vienna settlement had been arrived at by co-operation between them and the defeated French the inclusion of the latter in the deliberations of the powers after 1815 was considered a necessary additional insurance; the restoration of France to full membership of the association of great powers was regularized in 1818 by the Quintuple Alliance.

When it came to expressing in writing the intention of the great powers to co-operate, the year 1815, as is well known, produced two documents. One was Article VI of the Treaty of Paris, constituting the Quadruple Alliance. The credit for this document is Castlereagh's. The other document was the Act of the Holy Alliance produced by Alexander of Russia.

It is usual in considering these documents to agree with Grant and Temperley in contrasting the 'cold practicality' of the Quadruple Alliance with the 'warm vague mysticism' of the Holy Alliance. Yet both documents left nearly everything uncertain. It was not clear which of them was to serve as the basis on which international co-operation was to proceed. The League of Nations had one Covenant, the United Nations one Charter. The so-called Congress System had two covenants or charters and nobody knew for certain what either of them meant or which of them was to be the basis of action. It is not surprising therefore that what could not be done after 1919 or 1945 on the basis of a single document could not be done after 1815 on the basis of two.

That great power co-operation was possible at all was due to the fact that until 1820 no problems arose compelling fundamental decisions: though the amount of disagreement on basic principles that emerged at Aix-la-Chapelle was already considerable. But in 1820 arose the problems of the Spanish and Neapolitan revolutions. Were the great powers to act in these matters? If so, in accordance with what principles?

The answer of Austria, Russia and Prussia was provided by the Protocol of Troppau which was intended to be an amplification of the terms of the Holy Alliance. It announced as a general principle that the great powers should interfere, if necessary by force, to restore any government which had been overthrown by revolution.

It is true that this idea was neither explicit nor implicit in the Holy Alliance as drawn up in 1815. If the Holy Alliance had any political principles at all in 1815, they were liberal rather than reactionary. As first drafted by Alexander, it called on peoples as well as princes to regard themselves as brothers within the one Christian family: and only after protests by Castlereagh and Metternich did the Czar agree that his summons to brotherhood should be addressed solely to princes. But the real point is not that Alexander had changed from a vague Liberal into a reactionary by 1820, but that his change of heart made it possible for the Holy Alliance to be given, for the first time, a precise and practical purpose, the suppression of revolutions. The Troppau Protocol therefore, and not the original Act of 1815, is the basic document of the Holy Alliance. It was the spirit of the Troppau Protocol that caused the Holy Alliance to endure till 1853 and which prompted Bismarck to try to revive it in 1872.

The answer to the problem of Spain and Naples which Castlereagh provided in his State Paper of May 5th 1820 was diametrically opposed to Troppau and made further great power co-operation based on general principles impossible. He rejected the Holy Alliance altogether as a basis of concerted great power action and insisted that the only admissible documents were the treaties of Chaumont and Paris. To the question what were the great powers, acting in concert at a Congress, to do about Spain and Naples, he provided the unhelpful answer, 'Nothing'.

While one can have nothing but admiration for the cool good sense of Castlereagh's State Paper it is still possible to sympathize with the bewilderment of the eastern powers when Castlereagh made its general tenor known to them. For the terms of the Quadruple Alliance of 1815 had provided that the Congresses should be devoted to 'great common interests' and to the examination of measures necessary 'for the repose and prosperity of the peoples and for the maintenance of the peace of the State'. For Castlereagh to insist, in effect, that the revolts in Spain, Spanish America and Naples did not threaten repose or prosperity or peace, and that the suppression of revolutions was not a 'great common interest' of governments was to redefine the Quadruple Alliance almost as startlingly as the Troppau Protocol redefined the Holy Alliance.

From the moment that both Quadruple Alliance and Holy Alliance were thus redefined, hope of continuous great power co-operation was at an end. In future they could co-operate only on a strictly *ad hoc* basis; the search for common aims had failed. The normal, in future, would be the separation of Europe into East and West: England and France, as opponents of the Troppau principle on one side, Austria, Russia and Prussia, as its supporters, on the other.

What prevented this division from producing more than one open clash as the century proceeded was that neither side was ever fundamentally united. The Holy Alliance presented the West with an imposingly severe front against revolution; but behind the façade was the historic Austro-Russian rivalry in the Balkans, the central factor in nineteenth century history. As for England and France, their co-operation was based on the abdication by France of her position as an expanding great power. But since France could not forget Richelieu, Louis XIV and Napoleon I as easily as all that, Anglo-French co-operation was always liable to be temporarily broken, as in the Syrian and Spanish episodes in the period of the July Monarchy, and after Napoleon III's incursion into Italy. So that sometimes lifelines were thrown across from East to West or vice-versa: thus, England and Austria might sometimes co-operate against Russia, or England and Russia might co-operate against France. There was, all through the century, a gap between the political philosophies of East and West: but no Iron Curtain.

Yet the Holy Alliance as consecrated at Troppau was an important preservative of peace in Europe. For so long as it kept Austria, Russia and Prussia together, peace was almost certain, and war, when it came, only partial. The fact that the Holy Alliance had existed helped to prevent Prussia and Austria from fighting against Russia in the Crimean War, and thus kept the conflict outside the main European area, confining it to the Crimea, where nothing vital could be destroyed and no essential changes be effected. Its collapse after 1856 was the prelude to the destruction of the 1815 settlement in Italy and Germany: for only because Austria was isolated from an aggrieved Russia could Napoleon III and Bismarck create the new Italy and the new Germany (and indirectly an autonomous Hungary) at Austria's expense. Moreover, Bismarck's first concern after 1871 was to recreate the Alliance from whose years of eclipse he had profited. The Three Emperors League of 1872 was alleged, like the Protocol of Troppau, to be based on a common resistance to republicanism; and all Bismarck's subsequent ingenuity in foreign affairs was directed to the same end as the policy of Metternich, that of preventing Austrians and Russians from fighting over the Eastern Question. For only when that happened would a general European war be inevitable.

It may be objected that it is inaccurate to prolong the life of the Holy Alliance from 1820 until after 1871, and be argued that by the latter year the relations between Austrians, Russians and Germans were in no way governed either by the terms or by the spirit of the Troppau Protocol. But a common fear of revolution and republicanism was the only basis on which these three Powers could possibly remain at peace with one another. Their other interests, if transferred from the field of aspiration to the field of action could be productive only of their disunity, and eventually of war between them. Prussia wanted (in the long run and not necessarily as a matter of immediate policy at any one date) to become the paramount power in Germany. Austria wished to prevent this. Russia (again, in the long run and not necessarily as a matter of immediate policy at any given date) wanted control of the Balkans and the Black Sea. Before 1866 Austria wanted at least to prevent this, also; and after 1866 she wanted not merely to prevent it but anticipate it. Moreover the method of peaceful solution by partition, which Frederick the Great had so astutely devised to prevent these same Powers fighting over Poland in the eighteenth century, could not be applied to Turkey because neither Great Britain nor France would agree to it.

Therefore, if peace was to be preserved, the three Eastern Powers had to act as if they had one common interest which outweighed their rivalries. Fear of revolution, which was real to all of them, provided that common bond. So that the essential diplomatic achievement of Metternich was to bind his natural enemies, Prussia and Russia, to him, against this common ideological enemy. He successfully persuaded them at times that this was the major problem of the age. Perhaps his triumph was greater than that, for he persuaded most of the historians to agree with him, too. But grave though the threats of German intellectuals, and Italian, Hungarian and Polish patriots were to states whose very existence was based on a denial of patriotism and on the imprisonment of the liberal intellect, the real danger, as Metternich saw, lay in war. It was European war, not revolution, that overthrew the Habsburgs in the end. To prevent war, therefore, Metternich took his two potential enemies, Prussia and Russia, into the protective custody of an anti-revolutionary Holy Alliance.

III

THE HOLY ALLIANCE, EUROPE AND THE EAST 1820–1841

INDICATION that from the outset the effect of the Troppau Protocol was to restrain Russia at least as much as to suppress Revolutions is forthcoming with the outbreak of the Greek revolt. Throughout the rest of Alexander's life he found himself hamstrung by the principles he had propounded at Troppau. These principles compelled him to abstain from assisting the Greeks. They were fellow-Christians, they were suffering at the hands of infidel Turks who were also the traditional enemies of the Russians: but they were engaged in rebellion, and Troppau had made rebellion an international crime.

Metternich and Castlereagh worked together to restrain Alexander. This shows that neither Metternich nor Castlereagh regarded the division made at Troppau as seriously as they regarded the danger of Russian adventures in the Turkish empire. Had Castlereagh lived, it is possible that the Eastern Question might have provided him with yet a third foundation on which to build that Great Power co-operation which, despite Troppau, he still regarded as essential to peace. This was the principle that Palmerston was later to develop with such exquisite skill, namely that the problem of Turkey was one which should invariably be dealt with by all the Powers acting together and never by one or two of them acting in isolation. It was a principle which, as the Greek question eventually proved, could assist Austria to restrain Russia; or could assist Russia to restrain France, as was shown in the

Syrian dispute. If Metternich's Holy Alliance at any time failed to divert Russian attention from Turkey, the principle of international action, sharply enunciated from London, might yet save the day.

The establishment of this principle was however delayed, first by the death of Castlereagh, and then by the highly personal policy which Canning adopted over the Greek Question. It has long been insisted that there was no 'real' difference between the foreign policies of the two men, but this is contrary to the facts.

It is true that Canning's claim to have destroyed the Congress 'system' is largely of his own invention. It rests largely on the fact that Canning claimed the distinction publicly, and opposed general intervention in Spain, and all intervention in Spanish America, in phrases as memorable as they are meaningless. It does not appear to have been generally realized that Castlereagh had already broken the system in 1820, because Castlereagh had little ability at explaining himself to the House of Commons, let alone to the general public. Accordingly, Canning was able to pretend that his policy was new, dynamic, fearless and liberal. Yet his Spanish and Spanish American policies (as Canning privately admitted) were strictly in accordance with Castlereagh's State Paper. The only difference between the two is that Canning rejoiced in the failure of the Congresses, whereas Castlereagh would have regretted it.

There is novelty, however, in Canning's policy. It consists, not in his having dissociated Great Britain from the policies advocated by the East at the Congress of Verona, but in his policy over Greece. We have the authority of Sir Charles Webster for saying that the only certainty there is about Canning's Greek policy is that he sought to use the problem to divide Austria from Russia. Thus, whereas Castlereagh tried to ignore the Holy Alliance, Canning tried to break it, not so much to spite the Russians as to spite Metternich, whose ascendancy in European diplomacy must have infuriated Canning almost as much as later on it infuriated Palmerston.

Canning's policy triumphed at the Treaty of London in 1827, when England, France and Russia proclaimed one policy (that which led to Navarino) and left Metternich alone with only the useless Prussians to support him in the advocacy of a contrary policy. Navarino called forth from the depths of Metternich's soul the despairing cries of a man who sees a life's work cast into ruins; just as his earlier observations on the news of Canning's death indicate that he regarded that event as a miracle wrought by Divine Providence just in time to avert utter disaster.

There does not now seem to have been much merit in Canning's attempt to set the Russians against the Austrians in this matter of Greece. The consequence—and this was the theme of Metternich's melodramatic lamentations—would merely be the encouragement of Russia in a forward policy against the Turks that would be as much to the disadvantage of the British as to the Austrians.

It may well be that Canning's policy, which looks like an attempt to restore the Balance of Power by sowing discord between the powerful Eastern states, had as much of the purely personal in it as had the readiness of the new Czar Nicholas I to co-operate with the British. Canning did not want Europe to be controlled by Metternich: equally, the new Czar was attempting to extricate Russian policy from the tutelage of Metternich much as William II of Germany later sought to extricate German policy from the tutelage of Bismarck. It was a youthful restiveness in the Czar that made Metternich very sad: it was one more burden added to the so many he felt himself sustaining as the world's wisest of statesmen.

It was however a fair comment of Metternich's on Canning's foreign policy in the East that he had destroyed much and created nothing. His death enabled the Powers once more to co-operate. Wellington and Aberdeen had none of Canning's histrionic Liberalism. Through them the Greek Question was eventually settled by international action, and Russia was in the end successfully restrained.

Russia's failure to achieve any substantial gains from the war of 1827–1828 led Nicholas to revert to the pacific Eastern policy of Alexander I. This was due in part to a change of opinion in Russia itself. It may also have been due to the terrifying spectacle of the 1830 Revolutions. Separation from Austria, accompanied by war in Turkey, had achieved little positive, and had been followed by revolution, which had raised its head in Paris, Brussels, Italy and Warsaw. If evidence were needed of the accuracy of Metternich's view that war in the East would mean revolution everywhere, the events of 1830 seemed to provide it. It is not therefore surprising that the Holy Alliance shortly reappeared in a new form (though Prussia did not take part) in the Münchengrätz agreement of 1834. This made explicit what Metternich had been trying to imply all along: the agreement of the two powers to maintain the *status quo* in Turkey. Even if the treaty merely intended to guarantee the Sultan against Mehemet Ali, rather than the territorial integrity of the Sultan's Empire, Münchengrätz nevertheless represents a triumph of Austrian policy: for the wayward Nicholas was brought into step with Metternich again, in the matter of Eastern Question as well as in the matter of revolution in the West. If there was a Metternich system, its chief documents are probably not the Carlsbad Decrees but Troppau and Münchengrätz.

Palmerston's view of foreign policy was, to begin with, closer to Canning's than to Castlereagh's. For a time, however, he sought, not to divide, but to oppose the Holy Alliance. As was probably true of Canning, Palmerston's quite admirable dislike of Metternich's pettifogging policy of persecuting professors and his contempt for Metternich's idleness and conceit made him slow to realize what Castlereagh's clearer vision had seen at once: that in the matter of Russia, England and Metternich had the same aim, that of keeping her under restraint. Hence, Palmerston's first reaction to Unkiar Skelessi and Münchengrätz was the Quadruple Alliance of 1834 between Great Britain, France, Spain and Portugal, which was avowedly contrived as a liberal counterbalance to the Powers of the Holy Alliance. He called this 'the great object of our policy'. It was perhaps fortunate that this elaborate setpiece of Palmerston's proved to be only a damp squib. The problem of international relations was not some imaginary threat to the West by Austria, Russia and Prussia, but the danger of war over the Eastern Question, or, as Palmerston now began to realize, the danger of an Austro-Russian 'deal' over it. Seen in relation to the permanence and magnitude of this problem, Palmerston's Quadruple Alliance was an ideological aberration.

The real problems that faced Palmerston after 1834 were to cancel Unkiar Skelessi because it made 'the Russian Ambassador the Chief Minister of the Sultan' and to substitute for the bilateral Treaty of Münchengrätz the principle that the future of Turkey was a matter for the Great Powers in concert. This could only be done, as the event proved, by negotiation with Austria and Russia, not by hurling insults at them. It was by patient negotiation across the ideological divide that he had achieved his brilliant feat of preventing the Holy Alliance applying the principles of Troppau to Belgium. It was by a repetition of the same business-like method that he solved the problems of Syria and the Straits. In comparison with such methods, the Quadruple Alliance of 1834 was a blunt instrument.

Therefore, while continuing to damn the political philosophy of the Holy Alliance, Palmerston worked with it and not against it over Mehemet Ali. The change of front was made easier for him by circumstances. The first was that in 1839 the chief threat to the *status quo* came from the French. Cast as amenable lieutenants in his own Quadruple Alliance, they suddenly chose to throw common sense to the winds and to make themselves conspicuously dangerous and unpopular by espousing the cause of Mehemet Ali. Both the Quadruple Alliance of 1834 and the Anglo-French *entente* which was the essential part of it had collapsed.

The second circumstance that eased the way to negotiation was that it was Nicholas rather than Metternich that Palmerston had to deal with. Once more, personalities are important. Nicholas was on bad terms with Metternich again, and so Palmerston had the personal satisfaction of supplanting the Austrian as the conductor of the international symphony. Metternich by 1839 was not the Metternich he had been, either in strength of will or in political influence. The Habsburgs were almost as tired of him as Nicholas was. Between 1839 and 1841, Metternich's policy, apart from an unsuccessful attempt to keep the centre of diplomatic gravity from shifting from Vienna to London, seems to have been based on a paralysed fear of war devoid of any constructive notion as to how the crisis could be settled.

United therefore by a common dislike of the French and of Metternich, Palmerston the avowed Liberal embarked on a period of fruitful, if uncharacteristic, collaboration with Nicholas of Russia, the avowed reactionary. Out of this collaboration came the 1840 Treaty of London and the Straits Convention of 1841, which must be ranked with the Belgian Treaty of London as among the most satisfying diplomatic achievements of the century. Difficulties were sensibly solved by men acting as statesmen and not as pedlars of political panaceas. A peaceful outcome was achieved by the temporary obliteration of the division first made in 1820. Neither side was asked to compromise its essential political theories, or its ultimate aims: thus Russia would not agree to guarantee the integrity of the Turkish Empire, and Palmerston, having gained so much, let the matter drop. And all that collapsed was the inflated folly of the French.

Yet nothing is perfect in diplomacy. The Syrian negotiations appeared to convince the Czar that co-operation with England was a surer way to achieve peace in the East than was co-operation with Austria. This explains his famous conversations with Aberdeen and Seymour. His mistake was in thinking that such collaboration would be forthcoming for any policy other than that of maintaining the *status quo*. It was an error that harboured the germ-cells of the Crimean War.

IV

THE CRIMEAN WAR—CAUSES AND CONSEQUENCES

EUROPEAN peace after 1815 had depended in part on the successful use by Metternich of the fear of revolution as a means of hypnotizing Russia into a passive policy towards Turkey.

By 1853 the Holy Alliance had been gravely weakened. Its architect, Metternich, long in decline, was no longer in power. Its chief exponent, Nicholas I, who unlike either Metternich or Alexander I was an autocrat without qualification, had, after 1839, escaped from Metternich's influence and had shown a strong disposition to prefer the company of Palmerston and Aberdeen. Moreover, both Austria and Prussia were heavily preoccupied with the restoration of their authority in Germany, Hungary and Italy after the revolutionary turmoil of 1848. But for the Czar, the Austrians might not have defeated the Hungarians, and the new Austrian Emperor, Francis Joseph, stood in relation to Nicholas I not so much as an ally as a protégé. The disappearance of Metternich from the diplomatic scene had deprived the Habsburgs of their last lingering scrap of intelligence, and the Holy Alliance had thus become unbalanced. A Hohenzollern half-wit and a handsome Habsburg dimwit, both only nominally at the head of states but recently racked with revolution, were not so much a restraint upon Nicholas I as an incitement to him to adventure forward in the belief that they could do nothing to stop him.

The other guarantor of the Near Eastern peace had been

Palmerston who had insisted on the international character of the problem. But just as the Habsburgs had sacrificed Metternich to the students and the rabble of Vienna, so Lord John Russell and Lord Aberdeen had sacrificed Palmerston to the constitutional susceptibilities of the Prince Consort and Queen Victoria. Accordingly, among the causes of the Crimean War one finds the 1848 Revolutions, the decline and then the fall of Metternich, and the expulsion of Palmerston from the Foreign Office.

British policy was now largely controlled by Lord John Russell. His views on foreign policy were those of a Whig idealist, hating Czars as passionately as he hated Popes. Worse still, he was misinformed on matters of elementary geography. He advanced the odd theory that if we did not fight the Russians on the Danube we should have to fight them on the Indus; a view that ignored the fact that the Danube was not on Russia's most obvious route to the Indus.

Russell's approach to the problem of Russia was thus that of the misguided Palmerston who had made the Quadruple Alliance of 1834; not that of Castlereagh, or of Palmerston between 1839 and 1841, who saw that the path to peace was the path of negotiation, undertaken in collaboration with the other powers, Russia included.

Aberdeen, the Prime Minister, saw quite clearly that the method of negotiation was the correct one: but he was not in control of the situation. He lacked authority as Prime Minister, and he lacked, when it came to foreign affairs, that authority derived from the efficient mastery of his subject which had been the hallmark of the vigorous and clear-headed Palmerston. Aberdeen's sentiments about the prospects of war were as precise as those of John Bright, and his observations to the Queen on the subject express in more aristocratic terms exactly the view contained in Bright's famous anagram to the effect that Crimea was 'a crime'.

'No doubt,' he wrote, 'it may be very agreeable to humiliate the Emperor of Russia; but Lord Aberdeen thinks it is paying a little too dear for this pleasure, to check the progress and prosperity of this happy country and to cover Europe with confusion, misery and blood.'

These admirable sentiments counted for nothing because most of Aberdeen's Cabinet and most of public opinion agreed with the Queen that the Czar was a bully who ought to be taught a lesson. From the British point of view the war was only 'about' the Eastern Question in the sense that the First German War was 'about' Belgium. The Crimean War was based not so much on the Eastern Question as on the ideological breach between East and West first made manifest at Troppau. But all the great foreign secretaries—Castlereagh, Canning, Palmerston—had contrived to ignore that breach in the interest of both Near Eastern and European peace. In 1853 Russell was too self-righteous to do so, and Aberdeen too scared.

On the Russian side, Nicholas was rendered self-confident not only by the debility of Austria and Prussia but by his misunderstanding of the basis of the Anglo-Russian co-operation he felt to have existed since 1840. His excellent relations with Palmerston then, and with Aberdeen later, led him to assume that England was willing to co-operate to divide the Turkish Empire peaceably. But the permanent feature of British policy was a conviction that Russia must not be allowed to advance in Turkey at all. It was one thing to agree with Russia in 1840 that France should not control Egypt and Syria: it was quite another to agree in 1853 that Russia should control the Balkans, even if the *quid pro quo* was to be British control of Egypt. Unhappily nobody seems to have got the Czar to understand this. Had Palmerston been in control it is reasonable to suppose that he would have made it clear to the Czar, and in time, that the fundamental aim of

British policy was still what it had been in 1840, namely the maintenance of Turkish integrity—a policy which Aberdeen did not in fact greatly believe in. Then the Czar would not have walked into war bemused, as he was, by the mistaken idea that the English agreed with what he was doing. With both governments in no doubt as to where the other side stood, there might not have been, on the Russian side, an over-hasty commitment of prestige from which it was impossible to draw back. On the side of the British government, the nerveless confusion which led to the substitution of general hysteria for confident diplomacy might also have been avoided. As it was, given that the Czar had taken warlike steps, Palmerston was all in favour of resisting them. But it seems unlikely that the man who had negotiated satisfactorily with the Czar in 1840 would not have found means of stopping him short of war if he had had opportunity to do so in time.

From the French point of view, Napoleon III was like some sections of British opinion in regarding a war against Russia, the mainspring of the Holy Alliance, as at the least a desirable war. He stood for the restoration of French prestige, and for the refashioning of the map of Europe in accordance with the principle of Nationality. The Holy Alliance was Europe's defence against both these aims. A war against Russia would therefore be fully in accordance with the ideological programme of the Second Empire. In addition, Napoleon III wanted an English alliance. The chance of achieving all this when the Eastern Question was reopened in 1853 was so obvious that it came almost too quickly for Napoleon. He preferred to contemplate action as a matter for the future rather than as a matter for immediate decision. But once he had set off side by side with Great Britain along the road to war neither he nor his ally could withdraw. Neither could leave the other to fight alone in the greatest war since Waterloo, for fear of missing the proper share of the spoils and the prestige.

It seems therefore proper to agree with those who argue that the Crimean War was as much a war about the European balance of power as it was about the Eastern Question. At any rate, the experience of the Greek and Syrian Questions suggested that if the Eastern Question was dealt with apart from and in disregard of the general clash of political theory normally dividing East from West it could be dealt with without war. Thus the principle that the Eastern Question was international in character did not of itself cause the war. There had to be added to it the hostility of Liberal England and Napoleonic France to Russia on other grounds.

Moreover, the Czar, though he did not think he was acting with the general agreement of Europe when he marched into Moldavia and Wallachia, certainly did think when he pressed his claims in the Balkans in 1853 that he would have English support. And once Russia had withdrawn from the Principalities, no further excuse for the war, except that of teaching the Czar a lesson, existed. Hence the diversion of the war from the Balkans, where it made sense in relation to the Turkish Empire, to the Crimean peninsula where it made very little sense at all. This diversion meant that a war supposedly planned for the defence of the Turkish Empire became, almost before a shot was fired, an act of aggression against Russia.

Diplomacy struggled valiantly to avert the war, but the efforts failed for lack of diplomats and because passions had been aroused among all the protagonists, and prestige jeopardized too unthinkingly and too quickly. The value of Palmerston, for all his strident Liberalism, and of Metternich, for all his indolent cynicism, is clearly illustrated by the muddle and stupidity caused by their absence from the stage in 1853.

A full scale ideological war against Russia, conducted by England assisted by a French usurper claiming to base his authority on universal suffrage, ought to have involved Austria and Prussia on the side of Russia. Whether the war was a war about Turkey or about Russia's over-powerful position as the champion of Reaction, it could not be fought to a real conclusion if Austria and Prussia abstained from it. If the war was about the conflict of East and West, then Austria and Prussia should have fought with Russia against England and France, i.e. as fellow-members of the Holy Alliance against the 'Liberals' of the West. But if it was about Turkey, then a war against Russia to keep her back from the Danube was even more Austria's war than it was a French or British war. It is clear that Austria repeatedly tried to screw her courage to take the decisive step of fighting her battle for herself instead of leaving it to the English and the French: but to weaken Russia fatally would be to make Napoleon III the arbiter of Europe, to destroy the chief bastion of the Vienna Settlement and to unleash revolution in the Habsburg Empire. Also deterring Austria was the fact that Prussia was holding back too. Prussia had no interest in the Eastern Question; and to have fought against Russia in alliance with a Liberal England and a Napoleonic France would not, for Prussia, have made sense.

Austria thus had the best reasons for not wanting the war to be fought at all, and the best reasons for not wanting either side to win. Austrian diplomacy suffered a major setback when the war actually started; and yet another as the war proceeded, by its uncertain policy of acting sometimes against the Russians and sometimes against the English and French. It is as easy as it is usual to condemn this policy as futile. One sees diplomatic co-operation with the West in 1854 for the sake of Austrian influence in Moldavia and Wallachia; a reversion to sympathy towards Russia at the

Vienna Conference in March 1855 and a last veering against Russia in December 1855 by the dispatch to St Petersburg of the ultimatum that finally persuaded Russia to go to the Congress of Paris. Yet there is consistency in all this, if one realizes that it represented the necessary Austrian aim of restraining both sides and of bringing the war to an end as soon as possible. To pursue this policy of tacking in the midst of a war required consummate skill if it was to be achieved without making Austria the enemy of both East and West: that it proved beyond the capacity of the Austrians to do this is not surprising. The consequences are well known and momentous. By 1856 Austria had lost the friendship of Russia, never again to secure it permanently; but no compensating support was gained from England and France.

The results of the war, like its causes, are both Turkish and European; but in the main the European consequences are the more important. As far as the Near East was concerned, the Treaty of Paris was merely an elaborate pretence that the Allies had achieved aims which the limited character of the war had prevented them from achieving in reality. To assert that Turkey was a fully sovereign state which was capable of reform, and in whose affairs no other state had the right to interfere, was to pretend that fiction was fact. The Black Sea clauses could not be maintained unless England and France were prepared to renew the war the moment Russia felt strong enough to ignore them. These clauses constituted an intolerable affront to Russia, and may be said to have added to the meaningless assertion that Turkey was a fully sovereign power the untenable assertion that Russia was not.

The Treaty of Paris looked like a defeat of Russia by Europe. But by 1856 Europe in the sense of a comity of nations had ceased to exist (which adds piquancy to the fact that it was at this precise moment that Turkey was ceremoniously admitted to it). Austria was on bad terms with

England and France because of her equivocal behaviour during the war, and at the Congress found herself gratuitously insulted by the presence of Sardinia and by the patronage of that anti-Austrian state by Austria's presumed allies. And the Anglo-French alliance which had started the war, and which alone could have kept the peace treaty, had ceased to exist before the Congress of Paris had dispersed.

The temporary elimination of Russia elevated Napoleon III to a position of primacy in Europe, and that in itself endangered his alliance with England since the English had certainly not gone to war for the greater glory of Napoleon III. Worse still, the Emperor had already begun overtures to the new Czar, since he now decided that Russia was the only remaining European power worth wooing should he feel inclined at any time to take steps to remould the Italian peninsula. Accordingly he joined forces with the Russians as a patron of the movement for an independent Roumania, a step which the English regarded with the utmost hostility. From the French point of view the Crimean War first secured, but then broke, the Anglo-French alliance on which Napoleon III's international influence ultimately depended. The war raised Napoleon III to a height from which, since he could never sit still, he could only henceforth decline.

If England and France were at variance with each other and both were hostile to Austria, the old Holy Alliance was in ruins. Austria was now alone. The old unity-in-inaction with Russia over the Eastern Question having been ended, the situation Metternich had foreseen had at last arrived. Revolution was to break out in the West in new and menacing forms. In Italy a new and more resolute nationalism now arose, armed by Napoleon III and given intelligence by Cavour; and in Germany, Prussia, at long last, after two generations of coma, grasped the opportunities for conquest she had ignored since 1815. Against all this, an isolated Austria could do nothing but blunder from disaster to disaster, while Alexander II stood aside, determined not to repeat the follies of John Sobieski or Nicholas I, both of whom had saved Vienna and gained nothing but ingratitude in return.

The most important clauses of the Treaty of Paris were thus secret ones, unguessed at by the signatories. They provided free and unfettered opportunity for the destruction of Austrian power in Germany and Italy to those who had the courage to act upon them. Bismarck and Cavour were the chief beneficiaries of the Crimean War, and without it there might have been neither a Kingdom of Italy nor a German Empire. Not 1848, but the Peace of Paris, ends the Metternich era, for only with the Crimean War do those political upheavals become possible which Metternich had so long hoped to postpone.

V

REVOLUTION: ORIGINS

IT is idle to consider the causes of the various Revolutions in the period after 1815 without realizing that the major cause of them all was the French Revolution of 1789. Indeed, the search for origins should go back to the Boston Tea Party and the Declaration of Independence. Without them, there might never have been a Tennis Court Oath or a Storming of the Bastille, or a Declaration of the Rights of Man; and all history from that time till now would have been other than it is.

The American and French Revolutions proclaimed two astonishing facts, new in the experience of European man. The first was that men could wage war successfully against their rulers. The colonists had by violence freed themselves from the King of Great Britain. The French had by violence freed themselves from the House of Bourbon and gone on to overthrow or humiliate the ruling dynasties of all Europe. Such a thing had never before happened in European history. There had been wars between dynasty and dynasty, between turbulent feudal lords, between city-states and emperors, or between Christians and heathen peoples such as Arabs, Moors, Turks, and American Indians. But the idea that subjects could make successful war against their hereditary rulers was to open up possibilities in the field of politics as awe-inspiring as those presented to a later age by the discovery of nuclear fission.

The second fact, reinforcing the first, was that there had been formulated a political philosophy that justified this war of subjects against rulers. Not merely had the American and French Revolutions succeeded: they had been morally justifiable. It was this claim that they were just and righteous acts which removed them from the category of rebellion. Before this, the abiding belief of European man had been that rebellion was a crime. The teaching of New Testament and of Old, the binding force of the feudal oath, the theology of Catholic and Lutheran, the theory and practice of the absolutism that had prevailed since the Renaissance, had all so stigmatized rebellion as the ultimate civil and moral crime that only the most desperate of men had resorted to it; and they did so in the knowledge that society would regard as richly merited the horrible death that was their usual fate. This attitude had not been seriously affected by men's view of what had happened in seventeenth century England. The Civil War, even to Englishmen, was still what Clarendon had called it, a Great Rebellion. Cromwell was a regicide: and the only real difference between him and Guy Fawkes was that he had succeeded where Fawkes had failed.

In contrast to this, the American and French revolutionaries had claimed to be acting, not as criminals, but as standard bearers whose banners and devices proclaimed a new philosophy of man. They seemed to assert that all attempts to overthrow kings by violence were good, because practically all the kings of the earth were evil, and because the institution of kingship itself was evil.

It is not possible to do more here than describe in the briefest form the new view of man and society which provided the revolutionaries with slogans that enabled them to rally to their side men who in other centuries would have shunned them as criminals. By the time the Napoleonic era was over there had been created, out of the rationalism of the eighteenth century, out of the romanticism of the early nineteenth century, out of the utopianism of dreamers and the precise inquiries of constitutional lawyers, a galaxy of ideas as bright but as blurred as the Milky Way itself.

Among such propositions perhaps the most fundamental was the perfectibility of man. This proposition was more novel than that of human equality, since the latter was at least latent in the enduring heritage of European Christianity. The notion of man's perfectibility was anti-Christian and for that reason more revolutionary; for it is a basic Christian proposition that man cannot hope to be perfect in the temporal world, least of all when he cuts himself off from the Church, which is what most revolutionaries did.

The factors which alone prevented man from becoming perfect were the superstitions of the Church and the tyranny of kings, which between them condemned man to spiritual and temporal slavery. As Rousseau had put it in the explosive first sentence of the first chapter of his *Social Contract*, 'Man is born free and is everywhere in chains'. If the rest of Rousseau's Bible of Revolution consisted largely of verbose obscurities, the direction in which he pointed was clear enough for his like-minded contemporaries and successors. The end-result of proclaiming the doctrine of human perfectibility to a generation who were simultaneously told that they were free men condemned to slavery, but that they were slaves whose liberation was at hand, was the point of view which Shelley expressed and others acted on: that the world would be a perfect place as soon as the last king had been strangled with the guts of the last priest. It was to be as easy as that.

Equally new was the doctrine of the sovereignty of the people. There was no successful attempt to define either 'sovereignty' or 'people' in this context (or indeed in any other context, since in real life 'sovereignty' has never been more than a useful legal fiction, and 'the people' is, as a political phrase, not so much a fiction as a falsehood since it never means what it looks as though it means. No historian, however humble, should ever use the word). But that nobody (not even Rousseau, and he tried hard enough) knew what the sovereignty of the people meant in practice did not matter. The slogan served the purely negative but highly successful purpose of denying that sovereignty properly belonged to the rulers actually in possession. The failure to define what was meant by the sovereignty of the people made no practical difference at the outset; the great thing was to affirm that sovereignty did not belong to kings.

Similarly, all men were equal and all men were brothers. Once again the positive meaning of the phrases eluded definition, and their value was in what they denied rather than in what they asserted. They denied that any group of human beings could, by sole reference to inherited blood, or privilege or tradition or ancient conquest, claim rights over other human beings. Rights based on privilege and property and birth were no rights. The only rights that mattered were the 'inalienable' rights of man, rights which were his by virtue of his mere humanity. Again, what these rights were could not and cannot be defined: for the purpose of the idea of the rights of man was to deny the rights of kings and priests and the hereditary aristocracy.

These slogans, precise in their denials and all-embracing in their vast affirmations, proved to have the power to intoxicate whole generations. Only the tiny minority of families holding the most firmly entrenched positions of power and wealth proved capable of resisting them. Indeed, not even all the Bourbons or all the Habsburgs or all the Hohenzollerns or even all the Romanovs or all the Popes were capable of resisting them. A Duke of Orleans could salute the tricolour in the early days of the Revolution. In the next generation, it was an Austrian Archduke who presided over the shadow-play performed at Frankfurt by the German Liberals in 1848. It was another Habsburg, Maximilian, who after trying to woo Lombards and Venetians by kindness tried next to bring light and reason to Mexico. Alexander I went to Paris in 1814, to Vienna in 1815 and to Aix-la-Chapelle in 1818, as an apostle of Liberalism: Frederick William IV caught the contagion and so, mildly but astonishingly, did Pius IX. If such men as these could waver even momentarily in their support of the privileges and the philosophies of their class, it is no wonder that men and classes who had no stake at all in the old order should have been swept off their feet. No wonder they felt that this was a dawn in which it was bliss to be alive. Convinced that the vast burden of human wrongs, ancient as history itself, was at last to be lifted, they were ready to whirl themselves into an ecstasy of hope and into a fury of revolt.

If the new philosophy was intoxicating in itself, so also were the events of 1776 and 1789, in that they seemed to guarantee that ancient thrones could be swiftly cast down by a people roused to be resolute in their wrath. Thereafter the European mind was dominated by the belief that what had been done, not once but twice, could be done again. Amid the confusion and carnage of a whole generation of war; under the disciplines of the Napoleonic Empire; and influenced by the propaganda of advancing Allies, the philosophy changed its pattern. The kaleidoscope of men's dreams was shaken and re-shaken between 1789 and 1815 and by the latter year had assumed other forms: it was to be jolted into yet other shapes in 1830 and finally into the monstrous pattern of the Communist Manifesto in 1848. But one element was constant, from the day of the Boston Tea Party to the arrival of Lenin at the Finland Station: and that was the belief in the efficacy of revolution as such. The permanent legacy of 1776 and 1789 was not so much the philosophy they proclaimed, for that was re-interpreted and readjusted to changing circumstances; what was unchanging was the belief that social and political wrongs, whatever they were, could be put right by a communal act of violence. Until Marx at any rate, it was believed that not much violence was necessary, nor even very well organized violence; just swift spontaneous violence was enough, provided time and place were appropriate. After all, the Declaration of Independence had been issued not after, but before, the Americans had an effective army: the Bastille had been destroyed and Louis XVI's head cut off in defiance of Europe well before Carnot had become the organizer of military victory. A few brief hours, or at most a few days, of high courage, a fierce brave demonstration of the people's wrath, and the tyrants would flee and the new world lie open as all humanity's heritage.

When all the ideas of the so-called intellectuals of the generation after 1815 have been studied; when all the causes of discontent in France and Belgium and Italy and Germany and Spain and everywhere else have been analysed; when indeed the same function has been performed in relation to the ideas and the discontents of Europe and Asia in the twentieth century, the cause of revolutions will still not be revealed until one essential fact is grasped. The ideas and the discontents are secondary. The prime cause is that the years 1776 and 1789, and the events immediately following them, moulded hard and firm into the traditions of political life the notion that through revolution man could find a short cut to a paradise on earth.

VI

1815–1848: THE AGE OF FRUSTRATION

THE Liberalism and Nationalism of the period after 1815 represented a re-interpretation and re-adjustment of the theories of the Revolution to meet the requirements of a later generation. In order to rally the peoples against the Tyrant, the Allied princes had felt themselves compelled to adopt some of the enemy's slogans. They, and not Bonaparte, were the Liberators, and to prove it they came armed not only with swords but with constitutions, much as the Allies of 1945 offered Four Freedoms and schemes of Social Insurance. The purpose was the same in both cases: to prove that the Allies too had slogans, and to damp down social unrest by making concessions to current social aspirations. Hence the French, German and Polish constitutions, and the guarantees for the Belgians in the new Kingdom of the Netherlands. But since, after 1815, most of these constitutions were evaded, violated, annulled or restricted, the most convenient way of defining the Liberal version of revolutionary doctrine is to describe it as a desire for a constitution where none existed, or for the widening of those constitutions that did exist.

Constitutionalism was a restrained, and indeed slightly bloodless translation of the original phrases of Revolution. This reflected the brief period of respectability that some of the new theories had enjoyed under Allied patronage. It also reflected the recapture of the Revolution by the class for whom it had principally been intended, namely the bourgeoisie. The true function of Constitutionalism was to protect the bourgeoisie from the princes, who rejected the revolutionary slogans, and from the masses, who accepted those slogans but tended to take them as involving the sort of liberty that constitutionalists traditionally like to call 'licence'.

A constitution, by providing for varying degrees of representative government based on the votes of some sections (though not until 1848 all sections) of the population, for trial by jury, freedom of the press, rights of habeas corpus, equality before the law and religious equality, did make some men the equals of others. It was usually calculated, quite deliberately, not to make all men equal or all men free; but it could at least guarantee, if it was effective, the basic negatives of the Revolution. If a constitution did not commit the princes to accepting the sovereignty of the people in any democratic sense, it did compel them to acknowledge that their own sovereignty was no longer sacrosanct. If a constitution was rarely the Revolution in its purest form, it was at the least a powerful symbol. Men died for the Spanish Constitution of 1812 in Spain and elsewhere not because it was a workable scheme of government, but just because it was a Constitution, and therefore a standard around which they could fight with all the reckless bitterness that their accumulated discontents had aroused in them.

It is important at this stage to realize that in the field of politics men in large numbers act in response to ideas only if those ideas reflect their desires. Ideas give men courage to act by telling them that their desires are righteous, that their discontents are noble and that their condition is remediable. The attraction of Liberalism and Nationalism to the generation after 1815 was precisely that these ideas, if applied, would provide them with concrete benefits: chief among them the career open to the talents, which is perhaps the great constructive idea which the Revolutionary era produced. The real cause of most of the revolutionary agitation after 1815 was the general sense of frustration which characterized most sections of intelligent society.

The chief of these sections constituted those whom it is usual to call 'the intellectuals'. It is important, however, to insist that the label is misleading to the point of inaccuracy, and is based on a misunderstanding of foreign languages. Wherever the reader sees the word 'intellectuals' in nineteenth century history books he should mentally substitute the expressions 'professional classes' or 'liberal professions'. Here, Metternich is a better guide than English text books. He defined the so-called 'intellectuals' as 'Paid state officials, men of letters, lawyers, and individuals charged with public education'. Only by fixing his attention on professional men can the reader understand that the great practical end for which the age was struggling was the chance of a full and free exercise of talents.

The openings for men of ability in nineteenth century Europe were by early twentieth century standards still greatly limited. They were limited even in comparison with the opportunities already in existence in nineteenth century England. In industry, there were few prospects because there was hardly any industry, by modern standards. Millions of Europeans provided evidence of how conditions on their own continent frustrated their talent by deserting it for the United States where, thanks to the triumph of the Revolution there, they could find the opportunity that Europe denied them. Similarly, the demand for professional occupations greatly exceeded the supply of them: and by temperament those who sought to exercise their abilities in the professions were not greatly attracted by the hardships of emigration to the United States. Perhaps the supply of aspirants for professional occupations was excessive because the universities produced more graduates than there were jobs; but perhaps the real reason was that the jobs open to them were relatively un-

language from the one favoured by the dynastic family, or because they did not or could not disguise the fact that they were descended from ancestors who had long ago lost decisive battles or been transferred to alien rule by the accidents of dynastic marriages. Moreover the dynastic principle, while it permitted the French to be French, arbitrarily prevented the Germans from being German and the Italians from being Italian, condemning them instead to be petty subjects of petty princes.

The political division of Germany had become an obstruction to the ambitions of the professional classes, as well as a restraint upon industrial development, for which the Zollverein was an inadequate substitute. There would be much more scope for men of talent in a unitary Germany than there could possibly be (outside Prussia) in the small separate states. The *Kleinstaaterei* of the German Confederation confined ability within the deadening limits of a pointless provincialism: it bounded ambition within the confines of nutshells. All the highly organized administrative machinery of a large national state, all its innumerable political openings, all the opportunities it could provide for the exercise of the talents of lawyer, journalist, scholar, public official and industrialist—these things hardly existed for the Germans, and their absence was solely in the interest of the Habsburgs and their lackeys.

In central and northern Italy the same circumstances prevailed, aggravated by the presence of the Austrians. Thus the Liberal elements in the population of Lombardy and Venetia were denied the exercise of their talents twice over, once because the government was autocratic, and again because it was in the hands of foreigners.

Yet in general, these men of the professional classes neither made nor wanted violent revolution in the period between 1815 and 1848; and they certainly lacked the political ruthlessness to make revolution effective once it had started. The

Revolutions of 1848 were largely caused by the failure of Metternich and the princes who took their political orders from Vienna to come to terms with the professional classes. Once again, Palmerston saw more clearly than the clever European diplomats who thought him such a dangerous and irresponsible character. 'Separate,' he wrote, 'by reasonable concessions the moderate from the exaggerated, content the former by fair concessions and get them to assist in resisting the insatiable demands of the latter. If Metternich would only leave people a little alone, he would find his crop of revolutions . . . soon die away on the stalk.'

This was the method by which the English Conservatives saved England from revolution. It was the method of Canning and Peel. It was the method of the Tory peers who abdicated their functions by absence in the critical moment of 1832; the method of the Tamworth Manifesto, the method which, reshaped a generation later by the subtle fingers of Disraeli, enabled English Conservatism to survive into an age of universal suffrage, the method which only Carson and Bonar Law were foolish enough to try to abandon.

To Metternich, however, this method of recreating European social solidarity by an alliance between throne and bourgeoisie which could alone have saved the former was denied. In fairness, it must be admitted that it was denied him by the obscurantism of his Habsburg masters as much as by his own indolence. (It may also be argued that the professional classes were fewer in number and less politically mature than the English middle class.) Metternich once said that he was the enemy not of Liberal princes but of their Radical advisers. But he could not or would not make the distinction in practice. 'If you knew what I thought of princes you would take me for a Jacobin,' was another of those sayings of his which reveal that he saw what was wrong but either would not or could not do anything about it.

Worse still, the ideas of the revolution were being answered by a counter-philosophy. Liberalism did not have a complete monopoly of brains in the years after 1815. By then, Edmund Burke had provided European Conservatism with a political creed and Walter Scott had opened the still unclosed floodgates of intellectual nostalgia for the Middle Ages. The Right now looked wistfully (and myopically) back to the Middle Ages as a happy time when all power was unquestionably in the hands of kings, feudal lords and the Church. The appeal to history, made moderately by Burke, had become devotion to a myth. For kings, lords and priests had not been allies in the Middle Ages, but enemies, who by their strife had themselves created the very muddle in Germany and Italy that was now demanding solution. Nevertheless, in face of the common enemy of revolution the three forces did their best to join hands in defiance of their past. The device had failed Louis XVI in 1789 and was to fail again. But the reconstitution of the Society of Jesus in 1814 helped to give the movement substance, skill and devotion. It was a species of Roman Catholic Holy Alliance to match the Czar's Orthodox Holy Alliance. Its fundamental political aim was best expressed, appropriately enough, by the Austrian Chief of Police who said, 'His Majesty desires the purely monarchical and the purely Catholic since they support and strengthen each other.'

This other Holy Alliance produced catastrophe most quickly in the reign of Charles X. But it failed just as completely as a bulwark of the Habsburgs. For Hungarian, Bohemian and Croat notables were by the facts of that very history to which the Reaction appealed, not allies but enemies of the Habsburgs, and Metternich's patronage of their particularist Diets merely encouraged them to use the Liberal and National feelings of their regions as a weapon with which to fight the Habsburgs in 1848. Meanwhile the chance of saving the future by co-operation between the best elements of the past and the best elements of the present was being lost.

Not even now was revolution inevitable. The professional classes were constitutionalists and not incendiaries. Left to themselves they might produce riots in the days of their youth at the universities, but not in the days of their sober maturity. It is difficult to think of one revolution in this period which was either begun or completed by the professional classes. By their very professions they tended to the proliferation of words and ideas rather than to acts of violence. The Belgian Revolution was not started by the bourgeoisie. The bourgeoisie stopped the French Revolution of 1830 as soon as it started. They did not start the February Revolution in France in 1848 and they had struck the Second Republic its death blow by June of the same year. They barely counted in the various Revolutions of 1820, and outside Piedmont counted for little in Italy at any time. They did not start the 1848 Revolution in Vienna.

Palmerston and Marx, though the latter approached the matter from the opposite side, were right. Certainly by 1848 the professional classes were no longer revolutionaries in the sense of being devotees of force. And they were never revolutionaries in the Marxist sense because they held themselves aloof from the masses—as was to be expected from their middle class nature, and notwithstanding their humanitarian pretensions. The members of the French Constituent Assembly of 1789, saved from the King's armies by the mob which, unknown to them, was storming the Bastille, typify the middle class revolutionaries of the nineteenth century. The action of the mob assisted their work and was appropriated by them as a symbol; but it was none of their doing, though their slogans had encouraged it.

Revolts and revolutions occurred only when there were added to the discontent of the professional classes the discontents of the uneducated elements of society. These might include brigands and bandits as in southern Italy and Greece in 1820; deracinated cranks, ruffians and delinquents as in the 1830 Revolutions in Italy; unemployed or under-employed army officers as in Spain in 1820; an unemployed urban proletariat augmented by peasants migrating to the towns after bad harvests as happened in Berlin, Vienna and Budapest in 1848. The irresponsibility of students, the sheer incendiarism of fanatics, the half-lunatic, half-criminal proceedings of Europe's myriad secret societies—these, allied to the anger of workers in their thousands, and peasants in their tens of thousands, made the Revolutions possible, for otherwise the professional classes would have been leaders without an army.

The strange violent mobs were, if not actually called into existence by the slogans of revolution, at least encouraged by them, because these slogans, as has been said earlier, provided rebellion with a justification. It was these elements on whom the idea of revolution as such had its greatest effect. To the uneducated and the unbalanced, to the immature passionate natures of young men burning with frustrated patriotism or thwarted ambition or idealism—and still more to the starving worker and peasant—revolution seemed the only way. Not only did 1789 seem to prove this. 1830 in Paris proved it anew. And even when men of passion saw that the July Monarchy was not in the least like a new Heaven, there was Mazzini to tell them with the fervour of a prophet that revolution was still the essential aim. The July Monarchy showed not that revolution was barren, but that in 1830 the Revolution had been betrayed.

It is not surprising therefore that when the signal came from Paris in February 1848 the multitudinous discontents already astir since 1846 were exploded into action. The difference between the partial character of the earlier Revolutions and the universal character of the events of 1848 has various causes.

One was that a long period of indoctrination (or education) in Liberal principles had made the professional classes more clearly conscious of their condition and of their aims. This was particularly true in Italy where the writings not only of Mazzini but of the Neo-Guelphs had won the more reputable elements of society to the cause and had even created the dazzling mirage of a Liberal Pope. The mere passage of time, accompanied as it was by no sign that the old order was willing to compromise, had not, as Metternich complacently imagined it would, smothered the general sense of frustration but intensified it. To inflame Paris there was the effect of industrial under-employment made combustible by Socialist doctrine. To inflame central Europe and Italy there was the discontent of an army of disgruntled and hungry peasants; and if the peasants, the only beneficiaries of 1848 in central Europe, are given their due weight in the story, it might perhaps be arguable that the first signal for revolt came not from Paris in February 1848 but from the peasants of Austrian Poland in 1846; and perhaps also arguable that the correct English parallel to 1848 was not so much the fiasco of Chartism as the Irish and English misery that produced the Repeal of the Corn Laws.

VII

1848: YEAR OF FAILURE

OF the various reasons advanced to explain the failure of the 1848 Revolutions one seems to escape general notice. To succeed, revolutions need more than resolute revolutionaries—and not all the 1848 revolutionaries were very resolute. It requires quite exceptional incompetence, if not complete moral and financial bankruptcy on the part of the system of government it is intended to overthrow. Only governments who do not possess, or who are prevented by quite special factors from exercising, the will to resist are overthrown by revolutions. A certain amount of cash in hand, a certain measure of faith in their capacity to survive, a willingness to use the army or to let it act on its own initiative against the rebels—governments which retain these assets are not to be dislodged from below. Thus, not one European revolution in the nineteenth century succeeded without either armed or diplomatic assistance from an outside Power. In the end it took a world war to dismember the Habsburg Empire and to set up National and nominally Liberal states in its place. The aims of 1848 could not be achieved by the methods of 1848, for the reason that the methods of 1848 were those of revolution; and, in the circumstances that existed, revolution was bound to fail. It is a fair generalization that governments are almost always overthrown by other governments, and only on the rarest occasions by revolution. It needed the military resources of a world-wide coalition to achieve by 1919 what the men of 1848 expected to achieve by barricades and manifestoes. A unitary Italy, a unitary Germany and an autonomous Hungary, which were the chief aims of 1848, were only to be achieved by wars between some of the great powers and acquiescence on the part of other great powers. Bismarck succeeded because he had the resources of a Great Power behind him and the co-operation of France and Russia. Cavour succeeded solely because he had the French to fight the initial battles for him. What the Hungarians failed to get by a revolution they got in 1866 by sitting still and letting the Prussians win the battle of Sadowa.

The 1848 Revolutions failed because after the first shock, the governments concerned still wanted to survive and retained the means to do so. The Prussian army failed to suppress the revolt in Berlin when it began solely because of the temporary mental paralysis of Frederick William IV, who, like Pius IX, had briefly lost faith in the old order and flirted instead with the new. But the Prussian army survived the vacillations of its monarch, and when he recovered it acted as the instrument of repression over most of Germany until 1851. Like considerations applied to the Habsburg Monarchy. The simultaneity of the revolts, the spinelessness of the half-lunatic Ferdinand and the ageing feebleness of Metternich gave the rebels a series of local and transient superiorities which were gradually worn away as government and army recovered their nerve. The fall of Metternich gained nothing for the revolutionaries, and the abdication of the Emperor was their doom. For this created in the Habsburg Empire precisely that resolute will to resist the Revolution which Metternich and his master had been jettisoned for failing to maintain.

Thus it is unreal to assert that if the revolutionaries had talked less and acted more quickly and vigorously they might have 'succeeded'. It is better to say that had the Hohenzollerns and the Habsburgs talked less and acted more quickly and vigorously the Revolutions would hardly have progressed beyond the stage of sporadic outbursts of street fighting—that is, would not have become revolutions. For neither the Hohenzollerns nor the Habsburgs were politically and morally bankrupt in reality; they only appeared to be, and for only a very short time. The effective forces of order—the armies—everywhere remained intact and ready for action the moment their commanders could prevail on the governments to come out of their panic.

It has been suggested that the Revolution might have succeeded had the Liberals had the support of the urban masses. Since there were no large urban masses to call upon, owing to the primitive industrial development of central Europe, the point is academic. Moreover, where there was a large urban mass to call upon, as in Paris, the Revolution failed just as conspicuously. A more serious point is the failure of the Liberals to secure the support of the peasants. The peasant discontent of the middle years of the nineteenth century is still, it seems, imperfectly understood, chiefly because peasants, being illiterate, leave behind them no pamphlets and manifestoes on which historians may base history books. That in very many places in central Europe and Italy they burst into revolt and swelled the mobs who filled the springtime streets in 1848 seems clear enough. Their anger, fanned into flame by bad harvests and by the fiery slogans of journalists and politicians (and even by the sweeter breath of the occasional Liberal noble), gave to revolution in its early stages every appearance of having an army composed of 'the people'. But the emancipation of the peasants in the Habsburg Empire ended peasant support for the Revolution and indeed won them for the Imperial cause. In Germany there was no attempt to woo the peasants, in Italy perhaps no time.

Even so, it is dangerous to suggest that the peasants might have been able to bring 'success' to the Revolutions. It may have been bad revolutionary technique on the part of the Liberals not to appeal to them; but to say so is probably to generalize backwards a little too easily from Lenin's apparently successful wooing of the peasants in Russia in 1917 with the slogan 'Peace, Land and Bread'. It would be better to point out that the condition of Russia in 1917, when to an incompetent government was added the circumstance of a defeated and disaffected army, made revolution immeasurably easier than it was in 1848, when armies were fresh for battle against the rebels and were solidly loyal to governments ready to stand fast once the first shock was over.

An appeal by the Liberals to the peasantry in 1848 might well have unleashed a degree of anarchy which would frighten these essentially respectable people into panic-stricken flight back to the side of authority. Kossuth's appeals to the masses in Hungary led to a bitter cleavage among the Hungarian patriots; and the events of Paris in 1848 give no support to the notion that a revolution in which both moderates and extremists took part was likely to succeed. The 1848 Revolution in France failed as completely as all the other Revolutions.

An appeal to the peasants would have led directly to counter-revolution. The appeal to the National principle had much the same effect. For just as the slogans of liberty could conjure up the terrifying figures of angered peasants treating liberty as if it applied to them as well as to property owners, so the slogans of Nationalism, hitherto regarded as the special preserve of Germans, Italians, Hungarians and perhaps the Poles, were for the first time now being uttered by the Slavs in general; and the men of 1848 seem to have thought that the Slavs had been so deeply buried by history as to be beyond hearing even the faintest echoes of battle-cries meant for others. Once Czechs and Croats and Slovaks had added their competing claims for national freedom to those of the Poles and the peripheral Danes and Roumanians there was no hope whatever for the Revolution. Even had Prussian, Habsburg and Cossack armies not existed, all that 1848 could have achieved was an unending chaos of national groups striving relentlessly against one another and against the myriad historical accidents which had made exclusive Nationalism an unattainable and suicidal policy for European man. That confusion would have been bad enough. If it had been reinforced by a holocaust in which moderate Liberals were engaged in fighting off the demands of Radicals, peasants and proletariat, the result would have been as if the horrors of the June Days were to be enacted not only in Paris but all over Europe; and for months or years rather than for only days.

The failure of the 1848 Revolutions therefore lay in the very nature of the social situation. The revolutionaries did not understand the implications of their own slogans, nor the inadequacy of their programme. Small as the hopes of freedom were in the years after 1849, and bad though Cavour and Bismarck were for Europe, a 'successful' 1848 Revolution, in the sense of one that pursued a fully revolutionary programme, would have been a thousand times worse.

One problem which was neither Liberal nor National, but related solely to power politics, was also raised in 1848. This was the question whether Prussia could successfully challenge Austrian hegemony over the German princes. By sheer accident—the temporary Liberalism of Frederick William IV and the preoccupation of Austria with the intalern chaos in the Habsburg Empire—Prussia became identified with the Liberal and German cause in 1848. This leads to another mistakenly regretful 'if only' about 1848—'if only' Frederick William IV had not refused to pick up the Imperial Crown from the gutter, Germany would then have been united by consent and without Bismarck's 'blood and iron'. But Prussia could not and would not accept a Liberal and National Germany, because Prussia was not Liberal and cared nothing for Germany. More significant of Prussia's clear-headed self interest than Frederick William's refusal of the Imperial

Crown was the Prussian refusal to act as the agent of the men of Frankfurt in a war against the Danes over Slesvig-Holstein. Prussian policy in these two matters raised by the Revolution —the Imperial Crown and Slesvig-Holstein—prove not that Prussia was craven or short-sighted, but that Prussia was resolutely devoted to a policy whose watchword was 'All for Prussia or nothing for Germany'. The only practical issue raised in Germany by the 1848 Revolution was whether Prussia's assumption of responsibility for the restoration of order between 1849 and 1851 could be turned into a permanent domination replacing that of Austria. At Olmütz, Prussia decided to postpone the struggle, not to abandon it. A war with Austria over the Hesse dispute would have put Prussia once more at the mercy of German Nationalism, and Prussia held her hand. For their part, the Austrians held their hand too. The restoration of the old Confederation meant that Prussia was still in a position to fight another day.

VIII

LOUIS NAPOLEON, SECOND REPUBLIC AND SECOND EMPIRE

THE outbreak of revolution in Paris in February 1848 was an accident. To suppose that it took place because of Louis Philippe's unsuccessful foreign policy is, of course, wildly absurd; and only the most credulous will suppose that those who thronged the streets of Paris in 1848 were annoyed at the failure of Louis Philippe to offer them 'La Gloire'. Nor does the cynical complacency of the régime's domestic policy do more than explain the existence of discontent in 1848. It does not of itself provide an adequate cause of revolution. Revolution, as we have seen, takes place only when a government, faced with disorder, loses its will to resist. It was panic in a crisis at least as much as failures of policy over the previous eighteen years that caused the July Monarchy to be overthrown in 1848.

That the politically unenfranchised bourgeoisie felt frustrated with the constriction of power and privilege that characterized the régime is unquestionable. That presumably is what Lamartine meant by saying that France was bored. But a state of boredom is not conducive to revolutionary fervour; and the bourgeoisie in early 1848 were apparently so bored that they could not even muster up enough energy to resist the government when it banned their Reform Banquet. Whereupon the disorders were started by the proletariat, who were not bored at all, but very angry. And they and those who took their cue from them, acted not just because of their discontents but because of the revolutionary tradition.

The main cause of the 1848 Revolution was the Revolution of 1789 and the Revolution of 1830. Tocqueville, witnessing the events of the February Revolution, wondered at first why it all looked so familiar. Then he realized it was because people were everywhere striking just those attitudes which he and they had seen in representations of the events of 1789.

The violence of the outburst in the streets caught the 'bored' professional classes off their guard, and they found themselves landed with a revolution they did not want but which they were powerless to resist until they had themselves captured control of the police and the army. But the Socialists had got there first. Isolated by the collapse of the Orleans Monarchy the bourgeoisie had to co-operate with the Socialists and even let them hold the chief executive posts in the Provisional Government because the alternative was to be swept into oblivion by the raging Red torrent.

The bourgeoisie were thus never reconciled to the Second Republic. Nor did they ever quite forgive the House of Orleans for deserting them, for failing in its prime duty of preserving social order. A less complacent attitude to the rudimentary business of maintaining security in an inflammable capital like Paris and a swift resolute employment of police and troops were all that was required to prevent the Revolution developing in February 1848. In this, Paris was not greatly different from Vienna and Berlin. The failure of the Orleans Monarchy was primarily a failure of nerve.

The flight of Louis Philippe is the French equivalent of the flight of Metternich from Vienna. The June Days are parallel to the military victories of Windischgrätz and are the first act of the counter-revolution. In effect the June Days did what it had been Louis Philippe's duty to do in February—crush the Reds. But the monarchy could not be restored after the June Days, and so there existed the ridiculous situation of a nominal Republic controlled by an assembly of Royalist deputies.

From June 1848 until the *coup d'état* the Second Republic was a monarchy in search of a king. The Assembly was unable to find one partly because the Bourbons were impossibly demanding a return to the dead day of Charles X, and partly because the Orleans dynasty was unable to free itself from the charge of dereliction of duty in the crisis of February. The Assembly was also afraid of the effect on the masses of a direct abolition of the Republic. If the mere closing of the national workshops had led to the June Days, the abolition of the Republic, they thought, might lead to horrors even more ghastly. These factors, plus the failure of the royalist factions to come to agreement, are the sole reasons why the Second Republic survived even in name.

To men in so difficult a plight, the candidature of Louis Napoleon in December 1848 was a gift from heaven. He was personally innocuous, and if elected could be kept firmly in hand. He had no political party, none of the talents necessary for the acquisition of one, no personal magnetism and no powers of oratory. On the other hand, his name, and his authorship of *The Extinction of Pauperism* would make him acceptable to the masses. A President of this character would be admirably suited for the double task of keeping a place warm for the eventual restoration of the monarchy and of persuading the populace that it had in the seat of authority another Little Corporal who was also almost a Socialist. He was the only presidential candidate with a perfectly clean, because perfectly blank, political record. Accordingly, the politicians supported him because they thought he could save them from the masses; and the masses supported him because they thought he could save them from the politicians.

One of the most interesting exercises in what might be termed comparative biography is to study the similarities and dissimilarities between Louis Napoleon and Adolf Hitler. In many respects their careers run on parallel lines and a study of either helps to illuminate one's understanding of the other. They rose to power in a remarkably similar defiance of the laws of probability. They performed the same function of first restoring and then destroying the power of the countries of their adoption, and each destroyed the international foundations on which the Europe of their time was built. In lesser things as in important ones, they are strangely alike. Both were strangers to the people they chose to lead. Hitler spoke German with an Austrian accent, Louis Napoleon French with a German accent. Each had his abortive putsch and consequent imprisonment. Strasbourg and Boulogne were to Louis Napoleon what the Munich Rising of 1923 was to Hitler. And if Landsberg meant much less to Hitler than Ham did to Louis Napoleon; *The Extinction of Pauperism* combined with the Memoirs of the first Napoleon bore much the same relation to the origins of the Second Empire as *Mein Kampf* did to the rise of the Third Reich. They were both essentially seedy characters and proclaimed it in their looks. Hitler's unkempt hair and his belted raincoat produced an inescapable effect of back-street vulgarity: and nothing can prevent Louis Napoleon from looking, in some of the less flattering photographs of him, like a shady Italian waiter recently dismissed from service in a fourth rate hotel. And if the eyes of Louis Napoleon were rarely visible and those of Hitler inescapable, Louis Napoleon's eyes seem, while remaining half-shut, to have hypnotized the men of his generation almost as effectively as did those of Hitler which were almost always wide open.

Both had a gang. Both manœuvred into power with the connivance of politicians who under-estimated their abilities. Both sought to divert the gaze of the masses from politics by a concentration on material prosperity and by a calculated encouragement of public pageantry. The early propaganda of both reveals an adroit use of the device of stealing the slogans of the rival political forces of their day and pretending that they had found the secret of reconciling what the politicians had made irreconcilable. Thus, Hitler stole the Nationalist label from his dupes and the Socialist label from his enemies and persuaded both sides he was their ally. Louis Napoleon likewise offered France both 'democracy' and 'order', both social welfare and social discipline. He came promising universal suffrage to the masses, imperial glory to the army, Catholic liberties to the clericals, and an open field for profitable investment to the business man; just as Hitler simultaneously claimed to be liberating Germany from the monopolistic multiple stores while making it safe for the Ruhr industrialists. Finally one might observe that it was for not dissimilar reasons that the one built boulevards and railways and the other built autobahnen.

Yet there is an essential difference between Louis Napoleon and most other dictators and usurpers, Hitler included, which if clearly understood, provides the key to his character. Most men of this sort combine great ruthlessness with a daemonic possession. This was not true of Louis Napoleon. He had none of that fire in the belly that makes a man of action such as Napoleon I or Hitler, or even a Mussolini. He had neither drive nor organizing ability, nor the gift of steady application to routine administration such as characterized his uncle, or Frederick the Great, or Louis XIV; and his lack of the ability to come to a clear cut decision about anything is the most pronounced feature of his character. Whenever decision was at last grudgingly and uncertainly wrung from him he could only with difficulty be persuaded from going back on it. The *coup d'état*; the entry into the Crimean War and into the Italian War; the decision to take no action in 1866 and to take action in 1870, he regretted them all as soon as they were made, and endeavoured to go back on all of them, except for the decision of 1870, which proved fatal.

Louis Napoleon was a man whose tragedy it was to see a youthful dream come true. Many young men who, like Louis Napoleon, have little constructive to occupy their time with, dream of what they would do if they were ever to achieve supreme power. The dream has no reference to their ability either to achieve such power in reality or to use it if they got it. It is a dream that relates solely to their desires, not at all to their capabilities. Louis Napoleon obviously had more encouragement than most young men to dream such dreams, since he bore the Bonaparte name; but that name was his sole personal qualification for the practical business of politics and government. He inherited nothing whatever of the character of his imperial uncle; and scandal said that his mother could give good reasons for this. Yet, consciously, and with all the dogged patience of a slow-thinking (though much-thinking) personality he persisted in what by others would soon have been discarded as the idle dreams of a silly boy. Had he not been born in a Bonaparte household he would have found some modest niche somewhere—as a little-remembered princely publicist, a financially embarrassed dilettante man of the world, or as one of the more moderate deputies at the 1848 Frankfurt Assembly, a gathering exactly suited to his intellectual outlook and his limited ability; and thereafter, if he could have found someone to support him financially, a quiet decline into old age in the congenial atmosphere of London society, punctuated by amiable excursions to give improving lectures to workmen's clubs in the North and Midlands. He began as a political refugee and ended as one. The end was appropriate to the beginning; but in the high tide of his career he was acting hopelessly out of character. Few men have been more completely miscast than was Louis Napoleon when he posed upon the stage as Emperor of the French and the Napoleonic arbiter of Europe. It was a long time before anybody noticed how unsuited he was to his role, but that was because the other actors on the European stage at that time were inferior to him either in their intellectual ability or in the particular roles allotted to them. Cavour was a much abler performer, but his role was limited in significance and confined, so to speak, to the second act of the drama. Bismarck, naturally, claimed to have seen through the Emperor from the start, but Bismarck's conceit is notorious and the truth is that for all his ability, he did not dominate Europe until after the Second Empire was over.

Whether he was seeking power or exercising it, Louis Napoleon was irresolute, unmilitary, the reverse of ruthless, and devoid of that convincing air of authority with which some are born and which others acquire through the mere exercise of authority. Three examples will suffice. When it was a question of sending troops into the streets after the *coup d'état*, he panicked and left the job to Morny and Maupas. When Orsini's bomb claimed its victims outside the Opéra, Louis Napoleon wanted, like any decent private person, to go with them to make sure they were properly looked after. It was Eugénie who called him back to his official imperial duty, that of presenting himself calm and unruffled in his box in the theatre where the audience awaited him. When he advanced into Italy, the second of his name to do so, how different was the victor of Magenta and Solferino from the victor of Lodi and Rivoli. For the uncle it was the prelude to glory. For the nephew it was the prelude to a politically disastrous peace, made by a man whose visits to the scene of battle had turned him into a half-fainting, half-vomiting mass of misery. That his personal linen was freely given to be torn into bandages reveals his humanity as a private person; that the official bandages did not reach Italy until the war was over reveals his incompetence as an Emperor.

It is thus erroneous to think of Louis Napoleon's seizure of power as the result of deliberate and careful long-term planning. What looked like the overthrow of a popular republic by a military despot, or even by a shady political adventurer, was something very different in reality. Neither the act nor the man in whose name it was undertaken can be understood unless the difference is appreciated.

In the first place, Louis Napoleon's election as President in 1848 was miracle enough for him to be very content with it. That it was three years before he assumed full power reflects not consummate patience but a consummate unwillingness to make up his mind. He was Hamlet, not Iago. The avuncular ghost was doubtless always urging him to dispose of the Second Republic which had usurped the government of France; and in the end the deed was done. But the doing was far more the work of Morny and Maupas than of their leader. Louis Napoleon would have been well satisfied with the Presidency save for two things. It did not provide him with enough money; and it was due to terminate in 1852. But until 1852 loomed in sight with still no sign that the Assembly would grant him either an increase of income or an extension of his tenure, he refused to budge. His only positive reason for delay was that if he had assumed sole power earlier he would have been dependent upon the army leader Changarnier, who in fact despised Louis Napoleon for not overthrowing the Republic in 1849 as he could have done without difficulty.

For their part, the politicians of the Assembly had their anxieties, too. Elections for a new President were due in 1852, and what might emerge from and during a renewed appeal to universal suffrage was a matter about which they were profoundly nervous. They had no candidate themselves, and the restoration of the monarchy had ceased to be practical politics. They had many good reasons for wanting to prolong Louis Napoleon's term of office and it is probable that if he had really tried he could have got a majority in the

Assembly to vote for the necessary revision of the constitution. But he neither would nor could intrigue with the politicians, but only against them. Conspiracy was the only political technique with which he was familiar, and by 1851 it was clear also that a mere extension of his Presidential term would postpone but not solve the essential problem, that of how to stay in power permanently, and with an income adequate to his extravagant needs. Finally, there was the example of Napoleon I. Republic, Brumaire, Consulate, Empire—these were the stages in the first Napoleonic drama and the new Napoleon who was presenting himself in the title role of a revival of that drama had to fulfil the part prescribed for him by the historic text. Moreover, a lifetime of secret scheming with a few chosen outcasts like himself had fitted him to act in no other way.

Yet in a sense, although he manœuvred the politicians out of the seats of power, they may equally be regarded as having manœuvred him into the *coup d'état*. The members of the Assembly were too astute, and also too scared, to declare the abolition of the Second Republic themselves. They had killed it in June 1848, but there had been no death certificate and no public funeral, and so when in December 1851 Louis Napoleon brought out the body and gave it military burial he assumed at once the appearance of First Murderer. The accusation was to follow him all his life, and afterwards, to be elevated into an historical fact. By the *coup d'état*, Louis Napoleon did the Assembly's dirty work for them; but thereafter they could always assert that their hands were clean and that they had been staunch defenders of the republican institutions that the bloody tyrant had destroyed. The politicians, too, were as afraid as was Louis Napoleon, of how Paris would react to a *coup d'état*. The attempt might fail; and they were determined not to look in the least like his accomplices. It was this desire to reinsure themselves against the failure of the *coup d'état* that led them to stage the somewhat comic efforts at official protest which were made on December 2nd. It would then be on record that they had protested, but had been silenced by the military (brutally, of course) and haled off to prison. Having thus done their duty they could in due course make their peace with the Tyrant and lend their assistance to the necessary task of giving France once again the benefits of Order.

The full effects of proceeding by *coup d'état* were made clear by the events of December 3rd. Whether the anti-Napoleonic demonstrations of that day were cunningly encouraged by Morny and Maupas or not, and whether the afternoon's firing by the troops was provoked by the hostility of the populace or was a mere display of force by an army under orders to terrorize the city at all costs, will doubtless continue to be a matter for dispute. What is inescapable is the fact that blood was shed at all on that day. It made nonsense for always of the Emperor's claim to base his power on the popular will. As was pointed out later on, celebrations and pageantry to commemorate the *coup d'état* were conspicuously absent from the organized junketings of the Second Empire. Napoleon III, least bloodthirsty of dictators, paid a heavy price for accepting the role of a Man of Blood in December 1851.

For, in his career as Emperor, it is particularly important to see that the ways in which he was different from the dictators of the twentieth century are as remarkable as those in which he resembled them. His lack of ruthlessness was not the mere cowardice of a man with a weak stomach, nor was his guile simply that of an evil conspirator ever craftily plotting to seek personal advantage or, as the tag has it, 'La Gloire'. The evidence is clear enough that at heart he was a vague, well-meaning doctrinaire. If he was no Garibaldi, he was certainly no Cavour; indeed his ideas had more in common with those of Mazzini. This helps to explain the latter's rage at hearing Napoleon uttering theories about nationality, and interpreting the course of history, in phrases often extraordinarily like his own. It is also false to suppose that the Emperor had no policy save that of enjoying the creature comforts of his imperial position, much as he undoubtedly liked them. He suffered from having too many policies rather than too few, and from having policies which, like those of most of the left-wing doctrinaires of the nineteenth century, were inspiring on paper but vitiated by their imperfect and over-optimistic notions about human psychology. Napoleon III brimmed over with good intentions; to believe that he was nothing more than a sinister self-seeking adventurer is to fall victim to the polemics of his numerous enemies. Far too much so-called history about Napoleon III is based on the assumption that because he failed so catastrophically at the end he must therefore have been a very bad man and an exceptionally incompetent one. Yet in the breadth of his ideas, in the genuineness of his concern for Europe and the harmonious development of its peoples, he was a man of infinite generosity and good-will compared with the always cynical Bismarck and the often mean-spirited Cavour. They did not believe in the causes they diverted to their own ends, whereas Napoleon did believe genuinely in Italian liberation and German nationality. One of the many mysteries of historical interpretation is the rarity with which it recognizes that Napoleon III alone made Italian freedom possible. Mixed as it was with other motives (mostly concerned with the satisfaction of interests other than his own) his impulse to help the Italians was both sincere and exclusively personal to him. In all the evasions and equivocations and withdrawals that followed his meeting with Cavour at Plombières he was desperately trying to accommodate his personal wish to serve Italy to the interests and pressures against his plans which were operating both in France and the rest of Europe. In his dealings with

Bismarck he was moved by a simultaneous belief in the progressive and efficient character of Prussian administration and in the greatness of the German contribution to European civilization, a factor about which Bismarck did not care anything at all. His feeble compensations policy after Sadowa was a concession to French hysteria and no part of a truly Napoleonic policy. In considering his policy towards Russia, also, it is important to distinguish the fundamental from the superficial. He was the first crowned head in Europe to desire the overthrow of the 1815 settlement (a fact which rarely secures him the sympathy of the many historians who disapprove of that settlement) and it was for this reason that he thought the power of Russia should be weakened; not as an end in itself, but as a prelude to the re-organization of Europe on the basis of nationality. That is why once Russia was weakened by the Crimean War he sought an alliance with her. No longer a menace, Russia could be persuaded to support or at any rate acquiesce in his schemes for European reconstruction, schemes which were far indeed from the idea of another Tilsit with which he was credited in London. His ministers thought Napoleon mad to prejudice his English alliance for the sake of an independent Roumania after 1856; but his support of the Roumanians is comprehensible if it is remembered that he really did believe in nationality.

As for Mexico, it is not without significance that Maximilian was as infatuated with the idea as Napoleon was, and precisely because what looked like a predatory search for aggrandisement, or a 'banker's ramp' and what is generally regarded as a mere stratagem to secure Catholic support by reimposing a priestly tyranny on the Mexicans, was also the dream of a doctrinaire Liberal (indeed of two doctrinaire Liberals, for Maximilian was as full of good will as his patron). In opposing the Mexican clericals once he got to Mexico, Maximilian was, whether he knew it or not, behaving exactly as his thoughtful sponsor in the Tuileries would have done. The Mexican affair was foolish and showed a grotesque disregard for practical realities; but in its folly there was more good will than there was villainy or crafty calculation.

Finally, there is the circumstance that Napoleon III is unique among dictators in ending his career with a government that provided his country with more freedom than the government he started with. The visionary dream of a transient dictatorship for the good of the community to be followed by the abandonment of that dictatorship as the time of troubles recedes; this phantom that revolutionaries have theorized about and their opponents have derided as impracticable nonsense for over a century, Napoleon III almost succeeded in making a reality. It is much more a sign of his doctrinaire over-confidence than it is a sign of weakness that he Liberalized the Empire after 1860. He said at the outset that liberty would crown the imperial edifice; and the unusual spectacle of a political figure actually carrying out one of his promises has appeared so incredible that historians have been at infinite pains to explain the phenomenon out of existence. Yet to assert, for example, that in 1860 Napoleon III's position either in France or in Europe was of such weakness that it compelled him to seek Liberal support is to assert what nobody believed. Men as astute as Cavour and Bismarck showed no sign whatever of regarding Napoleon III as played out. They both behaved in their dealings with him as towards one who was the undoubted arbiter of Europe.

What makes the attempt at a Liberal Empire so markedly doctrinaire, is first that it was impossible and second that it led to disaster. It was impossible for the Emperor to convince the Left of his sincerity because of the ineradicable memory of the *coup d'état*. In her extreme old age, Eugénie insisted that the *coup d'état* had been a mistake; for it erected a barrier of blood between the Emperor and the republican tradition that could not be ignored. And if, at the height of her influence, Eugénie was a bitter opponent of the idea of a Liberal Empire it was because she was so much more of a realist than her husband.

For to set up a Liberal Empire was to ignore even more vital facts in French political life. At the most critical period in the history of France and Europe, from 1867 to 1870, the freedom of the press and then the setting up of Parliamentary government, unleashed all that was most irresponsible and tawdry in France. For the politically vocal French had opposed the Emperor's timid efforts at army re-organization for purely political reasons, and yet at the same time used the 'shame' of Sadowa as a stick with which to goad him into a war he did not want. Napoleon III himself saw no grounds for war in 1870 and did not want that war. It came about not because Napoleon III was then the effective ruler of France, but because in fulfilment of doctrinaire theory formulated twenty years before he had voluntarily ceased to be anything of the sort.

IX

NAPOLEON III AND CAVOUR

THE starting point of a rational understanding of events in Italy between 1858 and 1861 is a realization that in 1858 neither Napoleon III nor Cavour wanted or expected Italian unification. The achievement, by 1861, of an Italian kingdom comprising the whole of peninsular Italy except Rome, was something which though it happened partly because of Napoleon III and Cavour, happened to a considerable degree in spite of both of them.

The first confusion arises out of the meaning of the words 'Kingdom of Italy'. To all who consider the phrase after 1861 it obviously means the area ruled over by Victor Emmanuel from that year onwards, an area felt to be incomplete because it did not at that date already include either Rome or Venetia. But this is not what the phrase 'Kingdom of Italy' meant before 1861. Its meaning is best elicited by examining a map of Europe either in the heyday of Napoleon I or in the time of Charlemagne. It is at once clear that the establishment of a Kingdom of Italy, so far from involving the unification of the entire peninsula under one sovereignty could, on the basis of the medieval and the Napoleonic heritage, be applied only to some variously defined part of northern Italy.

It is certain therefore that Napoleon III's phrase about 'doing something for Italy' was even vaguer than it looks, for the word 'Italy' was susceptible of various interpretations. It is safe to assume that the Emperor's famous words were not intended to involve anything much more than the expulsion of the Austrians from the northern part of Italy; that they involved the idea of 'freedom' only in a highly qualified sense; and that they did not at all involve Italy's unification.

The creation of an Italian kingdom was, as it turned out, contrary to the interests of France. So also, as it turned out, was the creation of a German Empire. The dominating position of France in Europe in the past had depended on the weakness of both Italy and Germany. Nor was Napoleon III stupid enough to desire either of them to come into existence in the shapes they actually assumed. He seems to have wanted to do in Italy and Germany what Napoleon I had done—to create large French client states in those areas, and at the same time, though this was not essential, to acquire additional territory for France. The scheme had the additional advantage that in both areas the achievement of this policy would result in a diminution of the power and prestige of the Habsburgs who stood for the dynastic principle, of which Napoleon was Europe's chief public opponent.

It is therefore incorrect to think of Napoleon III as venturing into Italy because he was blinded by a romantic attachment to the cause of Italian nationalism. He took the action he did because he thought it was compatible with the extension of French influence in Italy. In doing something for Italy he would do something for France as well, and perhaps, if he could, something for the Bonapartes also. On the other hand it is wrong to think of his intervention as purely a matter of Machiavellian subtlety that misfired. The Man of December was far too much a product of his age not to share sincerely the contemporary dream of a free and regenerate Italy; and his entirely personal decision to take the first decisive move whence sprang the creation of an independent Italy has usually been treated with scant justice.

For in taking the step he did he was behaving in conformity both with the Napoleonic tradition and the Napoleonic legend. The voice from St Helena told him that the first monarch to espouse the cause of the 'peoples' would become the undisputed leader of Europe. That he should intervene to deliver the Italians from the Austrians was consistent with his self-chosen role as leader of the nationalities; and he clearly felt that in so doing he was placing France and himself at the head of the most powerful political force of the day. He and France, by co-operating with history, could secure the mastery of Europe's destiny by a great act of moral leadership which was also a piece of shrewd international statecraft.

Intervention was facilitated by the circumstance that it was Cavour with whom he had to deal. Alone among continental Liberals Cavour clearly understood the problem of power and that it could be solved solely by using the apparatus of power-politics, diplomacy and war. It was for this reason that he saw to it that Piedmont came to acquire this essential apparatus. He himself supplied the diplomacy, and the Piedmontese, often against their will, provided the armies and paid for their armament. But since the resources of Piedmont were small it was necessary to compensate for this fact by diplomacy of exceptional subtlety. Only by great skill would it be possible to secure the support of a Great Power and yet retain a reasonable measure of genuine independence for Piedmont; as it was, Cavour was widely accused of being Napoleon III's lackey and he was in fact far more sensitive to the need to placate the Emperor than is sometimes realized by those who are over-hasty to believe that Cavour was not merely an able man but a super-man.

Because he understood power-politics, Cavour was not a revolutionary. His spiritual home was remote indeed from the terrestrial paradise of regenerate nations linked together in brotherly love that Mazzini's mind habitually dwelt in; and Cavour hardly belonged to the same universe as Garibaldi, moving with the manly directness of a fighting pioneer from one camp fire to another. Cavour was a Liberal in the style of the July Monarchy, and had he been as French as his critics sometimes said he was, it would have been Cavour rather than Thiers or Guizot who would have guided the destinies of Orleanist France and have made a very much better job of it. Indeed there were times when his methods of managing the Parliament at Turin resembled those of Guizot more closely than those of Sir Robert Peel. As a Parliamentary Liberal, too, Cavour did not, like Mazzini and Garibaldi, believe in Italian unification. For him the idea was tainted with Radicalism, and his diplomat's sense of realities told him there were too many insurmountable obstacles in the way.

All these factors in his political character made him acceptable to Napoleon III who likewise was not planning the unification of Italy and could not prejudice his position by association with Radical insurrectionaries. In short, Cavour made the Italian movement respectable and safe. Or so it seemed.

Whatever else was planned at Plombières it was therefore not Italian unification. It appears that Napoleon III's plans were always fluid and the programme agreed on was always subject to variation in the Emperor's mind. A reasonable scheme would, he thought, involve the expulsion of Austrian influence from north and centre and the reform of the various systems of government elsewhere in Italy. Lombardy-Venetia, the Duchies and perhaps the Romagna, could be added to Sardinia to make a Kingdom of Italy large enough to be a useful French client-state but not powerful enough to resist the cession of Savoy (and Nice perhaps) or to pursue a genuinely independent policy of its own. Alternatively, Tuscany and the Romagna could form a second client state under the rule of somebody capable of substituting French for Austrian influence—perhaps the Emperor's cousin, Prince Napoleon. The Two Sicilies could perhaps be persuaded to become yet another French client state by replacing the unpopular Bourbons by Murat, yet another of the Emperor's cousins. The Pope would (somehow) be persuaded to acquiesce in the whole process by being made President of an Italian Federation to which the new Italian states would all dutifully adhere. All of the various interests concerned would then be satisfied—Italian patriots by the expulsion of the Austrians; Liberals by the abolition of ancient misgovernment; Victor Emmanuel and Cavour by the greatly increased size and prestige of Piedmont; the French clericals by the new dignity of the Pope; the French patriots by the acquisition of new territory and by the substitution of French for Austrian influence throughout the length and breadth of Italy; and the Bonapartes by the creation of new family connections in Italy.

One version of this never definitively formulated programme was offered Cavour at Plombières, another was actually agreed on there, and the last and most modest version emerged at Villafranca. Many of the variations upon it were no more than suggestions whispered into the ears of slightly bewildered ambassadors and those unofficial contact-men of all nationalities for whom the Emperor had such a great weakness.

As for what Cavour had in mind in his dealings with Napoleon III, it is probable that he was not fundamentally more precise and fixed in his objectives than the Emperor. The greatness of Cavour is like the greatness of Bismarck in this respect; it consists not in the undeviating pursuit of a ruthless master plan concocted in advance of events, but rather in the infinite suppleness with which he adapted his policy and his objectives to every changing circumstance yet at the same time remaining firmly in control. His famous sense of what was possible consisted precisely in being able to see clearly what was possible at each given moment. It is the ability to control a situation that is constantly fluid that marks the able statesman; and the success of Cavour and Bismarck is due to their possessing this ability, just as Napoleon III's inability to do so was a major cause of his failure.

All that can safely be said is that Cavour wanted to get as much as could reasonably be obtained, but no more. He certainly envisaged the acquisition of Tuscany and the Romagna, and although his great triumph at Plombières was to get Napoleon to agree to Piedmont acquiring the Romagna, he seems to have played the Emperor false about Tuscany. But his acquiescence in the proposal to cede Savoy and possibly Nice indicates how very far indeed Cavour was from being the apostle of Italian Nationalism as such. Cavour was far more concerned, and far more fitted, to play the role of an international diplomat than that of the instrument of popular Nationalism. Plombières thus only looked like a demagogic plot. In reality it was much more like an old-fashioned piece of eighteenth century diplomacy on traditional horse-dealing lines. Phrases such as 'the cradle of the dynasty' or 'the sacred soil of the fatherland' had no place in Cavour's vocabulary. If the Duchies and the Romagna were only to be had by giving up Savoy and Nice, then Savoy and Nice would have to be given up, and principles would have to give way to necessity.

Thus, it may well be that there was after all not much more deception involved in Cavour's treatment of Napoleon III than there was in Bismarck's treatment of the Emperor at Biarritz. And because no Italian federation resulted from Plombières, that does not mean that Cavour necessarily disliked that idea, either. True, if such a federation were to emerge, Cavour envisaged Piedmont as its effectual head rather than the Pope; but whereas a federation in Italy seemed a reasonable possibility, a unitary Italy did not, in 1858. And Cavour was not interested in the impossible. It is necessary to beware of Cavour's readiness to falsify the record after the event in the interests of his own reputation. Like Bismarck he was always at great pains to prove that everything that happened, happened because he had always wanted it to happen and because his guiding genius was in complete control of affairs from beginning to end. But that does not mean that he is to be believed when he says this, any more than Bismarck is to be believed when he says the same sort of thing about the creation of the German Empire.

The fact is that both the men of Plombières were deceived —by the Italians in general and by Garibaldi in particular. It was not merely Napoleon III's careful schemes which were swept away by Italian revolutionary zeal; Cavour's nice diplomatic calculations went the same way too. One thing about the Plombières agreement is certain; it is that neither of the two men who made it dreamed that they were inaugurating a series of events that in three years would make Victor Emmanuel king over all Italy.

As soon as the Emperor began, in his serpentine way, to prepare French and European opinion for his coming intervention in Italy, he quickly came to the conclusion that he had blundered into a trap of his own making. A man as meditative and as impressionable as he was could not fail to see how difficult it was going to be to limit and control the passions his intervention would inevitably arouse: the heady patriotism of Italian Liberals and Radicals, the justifiable fears of Catholics everywhere at this gratuitous patronage of the most belligerently anti-clerical government in Europe, and above all the furious determination of Cavour himself. Consequently it is possible to see reason in Napoleon's vacillations after Plombières. Right up to the moment of the agreement at Villafranca he devoted as much ingenuity to trying to get out of the trap he had fallen into as Cavour did in trying to keep him in it. As it was Napoleon all but succeeded in escaping; and was on the very brink of salvation when he was pushed back into the clutches of Cavour by the despatch of the fatal Austrian ultimatum. For when it arrived Cavour was about to accept the scheme for the demobilization of all the three Powers which had been proposed by the British and apparently accepted by the Austrians as well as the French. After that the Emperor had no alternative but to march into the hornets' nest, driven to it by the unscrupulousness of Cavour and the folly of the Habsburgs.

Despite the rashness of his utterances in Milan after Magenta when he appeared publicly to give 'the Italians' *carte blanche* to do what they liked, Villafranca was not a real reversal of Napoleon's policy, and not, even in its failure to liberate Venetia, a betrayal of the cause of Italy, if the phrase is intended to imply the unification of the entire country, for this had never been in question. Napoleon was certainly going back on his agreement with Cavour and on his promises made in Milan. But it ill became Cavour, of all people, to complain if, after the shambles at Magenta and Solferino, and with all Europe and half France hostile to him, Napoleon felt no longer able to fight Cavour's battles for him. If the Villafranca proposals dissatisfied the Piedmontese, they secured for them more than they could have got if Napoleon had stayed at home. Piedmont obtained Lombardy and Parma. Napoleon III gained nothing; not Nice, to which he had little claim, nor even Savoy, to which he had, on national grounds at any rate, at least as good a claim as Piedmont had to Romagna and the Duchies. Indeed, the really humiliating thing about Villafranca was that it represented failure for Cavour. Against the insistence of the Radicals that Italy should and could liberate herself by her own unaided efforts, Cavour had asserted the superiority of the orthodox methods of diplomacy and war in association with Napoleon III. And unlike Napoleon III, Cavour could resign after Villafranca, and thus appear to dissociate himself from what was after all the collapse of the policy on which he had staked his whole claim to be the leader of the Risorgimento. His rage is understandable; but in flouncing out of office he was not merely giving vent to his feelings. He was also pulling out on the partner he had himself chosen, leaving him to bear the stigma of treachery while preserving for himself the reputation of an outraged and bitterly disappointed patriot.

Moreover, though Cavour was out of office, Ricasoli in Tuscany, Farini in Modena and D'Azeglio in the Romagna had been, and remained, busily at work on his behalf, ensuring that in all three places the movement for annexation to Piedmont should triumph over all obstacles and silence every criticism. The Villafranca proposals to return all three areas to their legitimate rulers threatened to stultify their work. Yet the fact that these regions did not so revert was as much the result of the decisions of Napoleon III as the annexation of Lombardy and Parma. Cavour in fact went on negotiating with the traitor of Villafranca, and through those negotiations got the Duchies and the Romagna after all, and, what is more, Cavour insisted that the traitor got his price—Savoy and Nice.

If the cession of Savoy and Nice lost Cavour much prestige in Italy, it was a step which cost Napoleon III a good deal more. It wrecked his own proposal for a Congress to settle the Italian problem, because no Congress would ever give him Savoy and Nice, and the change of front increased his reputation for double-dealing and made him appear greedy for territory, which in fact he was not. It made nonsense of his appeal to the principle of nationality since he had no national claim to Nice. He could claim it only on the grounds that with Savoy it helped to adjust the balance of power in the interests of France; but the popular side of his prestige was based on the assumption that he, alone among the rulers of Europe, stood, not for the balance of power, but for the principle of nationality. The annexation also prevented his obtaining the renewal of English friendship he had sought by at last openly abandoning the Pope in the pamphlet 'The Pope and the Congress'; in this he justified Piedmontese annexation of the Romagna. The clericals in France were not more hysterical about this than were the English about the annexation of Savoy and Nice. To the former, their Charlemagne had become a Nebuchadnezzar; to the English the 'Alexander' of the nineteenth century had been revealed in his 'true' colours as a contemptible 'Annexander'.

Yet if the cession of Savoy and Nice was a crime, it was a crime in which from the beginning Cavour had been the Emperor's accomplice (as the English realized, though they tended to plead extenuating circumstances in Cavour's favour). It had been part of the original bargain to which Cavour had been a freely consenting party. If it was a violation of the principle of Italy for the Italians, it was a violation which Cavour had been willing to accept at Plombières, when he was under no constraint whatever. Neither Cavour nor Napoleon III had ever assumed that Napoleon III was going to help Italy for nothing. And to minimize the service the Emperor rendered to Italy is to ignore facts and fall victim to contemporary anti-Napoleonic hysteria in England and the sedulously cultivated prejudice against him that developed, after Villafranca, in Italy. The work of Cavour in the north and the centre up to April 1860 depended as completely on Napoleon III's initiative in attacking the Habsburgs as Cavour's later work depended on Garibaldi's initiative in attacking the Bourbons in the south. In short, the contemptuous attitude usually taken towards Napoleon III's work for Italy is one of the shoddier bits of the mythology of nineteenth century historians. Although he doubtless repented of it after the cession of Nice, the fairer verdict was Garibaldi's after Villafranca: 'Do not forget the gratitude we owe to Napoleon III, and to the French army, so many of whose valiant sons have been killed or maimed for the cause of Italy.'

X

CAVOUR AND GARIBALDI

IF Cavour had had his way there would have been no immediate sequel in the south to the war of liberation in the north. With the absorption of Lombardy, the Duchies, Tuscany and the Romagna, all that war and diplomacy could achieve had been achieved. For Cavour, therefore, with his fine sense of the possible, this was the time to stop—not as a matter of principle, but of practical politics. Rome and Venetia could not for the moment be attained because of the insuperable international obstacles. As for the Bourbon kingdom, it could be acquired only by war, even if Cavour wanted it; and as an astute politician and diplomat, he saw that an attack on the Two Sicilies was out of the question. It is not at all certain that he was much interested in the matter.

Garibaldi was interested, however; and unlike Cavour he believed in the impossible. He wanted Venetia, Rome and the Two Sicilies, and he wanted them united into an Italian kingdom under the flag of the House of Savoy. His object when he set sail with the Thousand was to get all three but he aimed chiefly at getting Rome and Venetia by a large-scale outflanking movement. It was Garibaldi and not Cavour whose policy it was to unite Italy by revolution from the south because diplomacy had made it impossible to do so from the north. Cavour said later that it was his policy. But stealing other people's slogans is a common habit among politicians. It is usual to say that Cavour encouraged Garibaldi in secret; according to some because he regarded Garibaldi as an ally, and according to others because he intended from the beginning to use Garibaldi as a catspaw. In opposing him in public, Cavour was, it is said, cleverly (and, to judge from the glee with which the story is related, rather amusingly) concealing his true aims by telling ingenious lies to confuse foreign diplomats. In other words, the expedition of the Thousand is treated as a more romantic and successful Jameson Raid, with Cavour cast for the role of a Cecil Rhodes; and a Cecil Rhodes who was not only fooling all Europe, but, according to some theories, also fooling his own particular Dr Jameson into the bargain. It is an odd comment on the view of international morality presented to the young in the history books, that whereas Rhodes and Jameson are regarded as rather shocking, Cavour and Garibaldi are paraded as heroes.

Not only is the interpretation at fault, but so, it seems, are the facts from which it springs. Cavour's first reaction to Garibaldi's plan was the reverse of what it is usually said to be. When the expedition was being planned Cavour did his best to oppose it, but had to keep his opposition secret because he was afraid public opinion would be more on Garibaldi's side than on his. Once Garibaldi had got away, what Cavour then kept secret was his hope and expectation that Garibaldi would fail. Cavour was glad when Garibaldi attacked Sicily only in the sense that he felt it would have been much worse if he had attacked the Papal States instead.

Cavour's dislike of Garibaldi's expedition had several causes. There was first the serious possibility that Cavour would get the blame for it and be threatened with the loss of Napoleon III's support, with a renewal of war with Austria, or some sort of general European intervention. He was also convinced that Garibaldi was a stupid man who was in alliance with wild radicals who would demand a republican Italy based on a system of universal suffrage. Cavour had no more desire to see Piedmont merged into a Radical republican Italy than Bismarck had to see Prussia merged into a Liberal Germany; and if Garibaldi succeeded in Sicily it seemed likely that Radicalism would go on to sweep Naples and the Papal States and threaten to divide Italy between a Radical republican south and Liberal monarchical north. Cavour was desperately afraid of such a possibility because it would have meant civil war in Italy, and a civil war which, if it came to it, Cavour would feel compelled to fight. The third reason for his dislike arose out of the irritating arrogance which is often characteristic of the outstanding statesman; an arrogance based partly on personal conceit and partly on a justifiable sense of his own great ability. Garibaldi was so much his antithesis that Cavour could not believe that when Garibaldi said he was fighting in the cause of Victor Emmanuel that was just what he meant. Cavour could not believe that Garibaldi's break with the republican Mazzini was real. He persisted throughout 1860 in treating Garibaldi as if he were a Mazzinian republican and for that reason tried without success, but quite irrelevantly, to get Mazzini arrested. Much of this has its unworthy side. Cavour, bitterly unpopular as the man who had traitorously given Nice and Savoy to Napoleon III, could not bear the possibility of being odiously and publicly contrasted with one whom the simple people saw as their saviour. There was not room in Italy for both of these men. The fact that Garibaldi as well as Cavour realized this in the end saved much bloodshed in Italy.

Contrary to Cavour's expectations and hopes, Garibaldi succeeded in Sicily. Cavour's aim at once was to get Sicily annexed to Piedmont. Garibaldi wanted annexation too, but not before he had reached Rome. He calculated that once Sicily passed into Piedmontese control he would be unable to use it as he intended to use it, namely as the supply base for his attack on Naples and Rome. This was precisely why Cavour wanted Sicily annexed forthwith, and why Garibaldi would not agree. Another reason for delay imposed itself. Sicilians wanted to be free of the Bourbons and of Naples, but hardly any of them wanted annexation to Piedmont. Incorporation into a Kingdom of all Italy they might agree to: but that would be possible only when such a kingdom existed—after and not before Garibaldi had proclaimed it from Rome, its true capital. Another complication was that Cavour could not simply grab Sicily. It was the property of the Bourbon government in Naples; and as a diplomat Cavour realized he had to be careful. The English, true, had no objections; but Napoleon III demanded a plebiscite, so that there could be a public appeal from the law of nations to the higher principle of nationality. Yet, since hardly anybody in Sicily could read, hardly anybody wanted annexation to Piedmont, and nobody would do anything against the wishes of Garibaldi (who was already at the gates of Naples and might soon be in Rome) an early plebiscite was impossible. In an atmosphere of confusion and rather unnecessary ill-will, Cavour worked from the remote distance of Turin to get control of a situation for which he was entirely unprepared.

The problems of the Naples and the Papal States, which developed simultaneously, produced an open quarrel between Cavour and Garibaldi. It was a quarrel which Cavour worked up deliberately into a public quarrel between the South and the North, and between the Liberals and the Radicals. And it was a quarrel so bitter as to make civil war the probable outcome unless it was averted by the capitulation of the South to the North, of the Radicals to the Liberals, and, above all, by the capitulation of Garibaldi to Cavour. In goading Garibaldi into opposition to him, in diverting opinion in northern Italy from admiration of Garibaldi into detestation of him, in capturing the fruits of a Radical victory in the south for the Liberal industrialists and middle classes of the north, Cavour showed great skill, great unscrupulousness, much mean-spiritedness and at times much short-sightedness. Yet in bringing the hostility of the two main forces in Italian life into the clear light of day and in producing a speedy short-term solution of them, Cavour deserved well of his country.

The questions raised by Garibaldi's arrival in Naples and the prospect of his attacking Rome were fundamental ones and had to be answered. Who was to rule Italy? Was it to be Victor Emmanuel or was it to be Garibaldi? Garibaldi always said it should be Victor Emmanuel; but if the crown of all Italy was to be given to Victor Emmanuel by the Dictator of Sicily and Naples, then the dynasty would be the prisoner of the Radicals who supported Garibaldi, and the politically and industrially more advanced North would, thanks to universal suffrage, be at the mercy of the backward and illiterate South. Nor must it be forgotten that in any constructive sense of the word the Radicals had no policy at all. With them, as with Marx, the revolution was all. Once it was achieved, policy was hardly necessary; heaven would lie all around the successful revolutionaries and they would need to do nothing much more strenuous than bask in the sunshine of perfected brotherhood. Cavour knew better, and on this issue of Liberalism versus Radicalism, he was right and the Radicals were wrong.

Worse still, Garibaldi would not want to stop, even at Rome. He demanded more than Piedmontese acquiescence in an invasion of Rome; immediately after that he would demand an attack on Venetia. Garibaldi's programme meant the prospect of war against all Europe. Thus, there is no doubt that the flaunting of Italian Nationalism on such a scale would produce an upsurge of German Nationalism. For though when nationality spoke with an Italian accent it said that Venetia was Italian, when it spoke with a German accent, it could say, appealing to history, that Venetia, like Lombardy, was German.

Cavour overcame Garibaldi by a series of astute moves,

some more successful than others. His biggest failure was the attempt to organize a Liberal revolt in Naples to anticipate Garibaldi's arrival. In doing this, Cavour was simultaneously trying to overthrow the Bourbons while maintaining normal diplomatic relations with them, and trying to thwart Garibaldi while keeping up an appearance of friendly admiration for him. The Neapolitans showed no inclination whatever to 'liberate' themselves, however. To the disgust of the Piedmontese the nobility of Naples fled and the rest of the population just waited for Garibaldi. Cavour's most famous and most successful manœuvre was the invasion of the Papal States, though here again he was irritated by the extreme difficulty of engineering even an appearance of a popular rising to justify a Piedmontese invasion. Indeed, the chief characteristic of the mass of the population in the Centre and the South in 1860 was their unwillingness to do anything to cast off the dreadful yoke of tyranny and obscurantism under which they were said to be suffering. As for union with the House of Savoy, its almost only consistent advocate, paradoxically enough, was Garibaldi himself, whose attitude to Cavour was first that he was a sympathizer and then that he was a coward whom public opinion and perhaps Victor Emmanuel would shortly sweep from office.

The Piedmontese invasion of the Papal States was not merely a wise statesman's method of minimizing the rashness of a headstrong collaborator. Cavour took this step for the purpose of taking the Risorgimento completely out of Garibaldi's hands and placing it once more under the control of Cavour and the Piedmontese. By now, indeed, the Piedmontese were beginning to be alarmed by Garibaldi's successes. He controlled as much Italian territory as did Victor Emmanuel, and it was easy to persuade them to rationalize their pique at this state of affairs by representing Garibaldi to them as a 'wild beast' and a republican revolutionary. So delighted were northerners at the Piedmontese invasion of Papal territory that for one wild moment some of them believed that Cavour's object was to capture Rome ahead of Garibaldi rather than to preserve Rome intact. Cavour made no effort to disillusion them; like Bismarck he often gained much by allowing people to go on misunderstanding him. For he simultaneously gained popularity with those who did realize his real purpose; for many Piedmontese did not relish the prospect of Turin ceasing to be the capital of the Italian kingdom and therefore did not want Rome to be taken.

The invasions of the Papal States and of Naples were acts of what the twentieth century disapprovingly calls 'unprovoked aggression'. Moreover, they even lacked the excuse so often made for such acts, that of being inspired by the noble aim of national union or the liberation of the inhabitants of the states being violated. Not only were the inhabitants of the Papal States and Naples without any great desire to be liberated by Cavour; he had not even wanted their liberation himself. Garibaldi had forced his hand, and there is much to be said for the view that Cavour united the Italian peninsula in 1861 less to please the Italians than to spite Garibaldi. Cavour's intervention in the Papal States and Naples was as anti-revolutionary in its subtle way as the previous interventions ordered by Metternich. Yet what Cavour did was to keep the foreigner out of Italy at a highly critical moment. By saving Rome from the Italian Radicals, Cavour secured the acquiescence of Napoleon III in Piedmontese absorption of the Papal states; and by settling the matter without active assistance from the French he secured the unqualified approval of the anti-clerical government of England.

The mere news that the Piedmontese were on their way caused great confusion in Naples. Garibaldi lacked the ability or the will to organize an effective opposition to the Piedmontese and most people therefore felt that they had no alternative but to bow to the inevitable. After all, Garibaldi had always proclaimed himself the loyal servant of Victor Emmanuel. The alternative to his abdication of authority was civil war, and for Garibaldi that was unthinkable. He would not do in 1861 what in a not dissimilar situation Cromwell had done in 1647, namely accuse the nominal leaders of his cause of being false to the Truth and then summon his soldiers to turn their arms against those whose agents they had been. Yet his dreams for Italy were hardly less impracticable than Cromwell's dream of an England ruled by the Saints. His absolute control over the hearts of his followers had been greater than Cromwell's, and the effect of his generalship on the destinies of the Risorgimento were far more decisive than the effect of Cromwell's on the Great Rebellion. Garibaldi's abandonment of his authority in 1861 ought in itself to have disposed of the criticism that he was merely a wild man. He was a great soldier and an inspiring leader of men; those who opposed him had so little of these qualities themselves that they failed altogether to understand him. They saw him merely as a distorted version of themselves, as yet another politician, but one who, because he got results faster than they and secured the uncritical admiration of ordinary people, must be branded as a dangerous rival with whom no compromise was possible.

Yet the Italian politicians—Cavour and his successors—may be forgiven much of their mistrust of Garibaldi. For it was much easier to retire to Caprera with a bag of seedcorn than to have to deal with the Italian situation his zeal had created. For the plain fact was that in 1860 Italy was not ready for unification under Piedmont, and Piedmont was neither ready nor fitted for the responsibilities of governing a unified Italy. If Cavour and the Piedmontese must bear a large proportion of the blame for the disappointments that mark the early history of the Italian kingdom, Garibaldi has his responsibili-

ITALY, 1859-61
SWITZERLAND
AUSTRIAN
EMPIRE
SAVOY
(1859)
LOMBARDY
Milan
VENETIA
Venice
FRANCE
PIEDMONT
PARMA
MODENA
ROMAGNA
NICE
TURKISH
EMPIRE
Florence
TUSCANY
PAPAL
STATES
UMBRIA
CORSICA
(Fr.)
Rome
Naples
KINGDOM
OF
NAPLES
SARDINIA
Kingdom of Sardinia
Ceded from Sardinia
to France, 1860
Austrian
Unified in 1860

ties in the matter also. The revolutionary attempt to steal a march on history, to force the pace of human change in the interests of passionately held beliefs and theories, is always a mistake. The human mind is capable of just so much change and no more: it can never willingly move as fast as idealists want it to. Under the impulse of extravagant hopes and mass enthusiasm men can move very fast at revolutionary epochs; but the hopes and the enthusiasm are so much spiritual benzedrine and speedily produce a contrary reaction. The aftermath is mental disillusionment and social disarray. Garibaldi forced the pace in 1860; but it was a pace that all but killed the spirit of the Risorgimento in Italy.

The centre and south were not ready for unification, and the plebiscites in favour of annexation to the house of Savoy proved only certain negative propositions. The enormous number of voters who said 'yes' to annexation by Piedmont said so because to vote against it was, in the circumstances of 1860, a vote without meaning, a vote for the impossible. It could imply nothing more than a wish to continue the prevailing confusion of an interregnum that could easily develop into anarchy and civil war. All the plebiscites really proved was that people were tired of the uncertainty that had prevailed since Garibaldi's first landing in Sicily, and therefore preferred annexation as the only visible means of getting settled government again. As to the sort of settled government they would prefer, the plebiscites gave them no chance to express an opinion about that. What is more, Cavour was determined at all costs that no chance to express an opinion should be permitted. Consequently the votes in the plebiscites represented not a rational decision in favour of anything, but a sort of emotional *te deum* proclaiming a general sense of thankfulness that the time of troubles was at an end.

Unhappily the troubles were not at an end. The real troubles of southern Italy and Sicily were not political but social and economic. Poverty, illiteracy and a great shortage of land; these were the essential facts of the situation. And since the Bourbons had not invented these facts, the departure of the Bourbons did not alter them. Worse still, the assimilation of the south to the Piedmontese system did not merely fail to settle the fundamental problems of the south; it made them worse. The most obvious immediate consequences of the Risorgimento in the south, and the creation of a Kingdom of all Italy, were conscription, higher taxation, an increased cost of living, and a brand new legal system centred upon Turin. Within a matter of weeks after the plebiscites, great tides of opinion in the south had turned against Victor Emmanuel and Piedmont; and the outstanding feature of southern Italy after 1860 was uncontrollable and widespread brigandage, combining the characteristics of a peasants' revolt and a Bourbon counter-revolution. Only if words are used in the narrowest and most legalistic sense is it permissible to say that Italy was united in 1860; for the new régime was rejected spiritually and politically by the more pious Catholics, and rejected physically to the point of open warfare by the southern peasants.

These perhaps inevitable consequences of the rapid annexation of the south by Piedmont were due to the fact that Garibaldi had forced the hand of the Piedmontese too. Cavour knew nothing of the south of Italy and did not even dare to show his face in liberated Naples. He and his agents were quite unfitted to the task of governing the south with sympathy or even intelligence. It was all very well for Garibaldi to hand his territories over to the *re galantuomo* and then go off to Caprera; but it was Cavour and his successors who were to have to manage these territories. Garibaldi had the satisfaction of doing his duty; Victor Emmanuel had the satisfaction of being the first king of all Italy. But it was Cavour who was left holding the baby; and if he and his successors did the job badly at least they have the excuse that it was Garibaldi's baby, not theirs.

Various expressions used by leading figures in Piedmont in 1860 indicate the state of mind in which the Piedmontese approached the problem of governing the south. The Neapolitans were 'canaille'; they were 'barbarians who cared little for liberty'; Naples was 'rotten to the marrow', it was an Augean stable, and it was 'not Italy, but Africa'. And the Piedmontese knew so little of economic realities that they were convinced that there was great wealth in the south and that all that was wrong was the shiftless character of the Neapolitans. For the great weakness of Cavour's Liberalism, like most Liberalism, (and theoretical Socialism also) was that it was cursed with an urban parochialism of mind. It neither understood nor cared for the problems of backward, rural societies: its entire philosophy reflected the needs of ambitious metropolitan man, whether he was a would-be industrialist, an aspiring member of the professional classes, or a progressively minded aristocrat who saw in an attack on the old feudal and ecclesiastical system more opportunity for the increase of his own wealth and power than he could get by defending that system. Free institutions, free trade, unrestricted opportunities for the commercial, industrial and professional middle class—these were the aims of Cavour and his allies, and these alone. Moreover, they were aims which were put in jeopardy by Garibaldi's policy of war and still more war, of revolution through the common people. Rigidly and rightly proud of their superior efficiency, pharisaically conscious of being in the van of progress, the Piedmontese Liberals were contemptuous of the people of the south for their ignorance, hostile to their religious feelings, and convinced that their low standard of living was due to their incorrigible idleness rather than to the intractability of nature. Granted that only the Piedmontese possessed adequate administrative training, and therefore had to govern the South because there were few indigenous administrators of experience, it is still unfortunate that Piedmont treated the people of the south with the arrogance of conquerors imposing alien institutions on a tribe of barbarians for their own good.

The effect of realizing that Italian unification could not have been begun without Napoleon III and would not have been completed without Garibaldi is to require a reassessment of the character of Cavour. If he is regarded as the resolute planner of Italy's unification from 1858 onwards, then the indictment against him on the grounds of his breaches of elementary political morality is a heavy one. Deliberate warmongering and calculated falsehood are characteristic of him. The fomentation of plots designed to disrupt the governments of neighbouring states from within creates an alarming parallel between his treatment of the other states of Italy and Hitler's treatment of the other states of Europe. If he instigated Garibaldi's attack on Sicily he foreshadows Cecil Rhodes; if he genuinely supported Garibaldi once the expedition was making headway, then he is not altogether unlike Mussolini encouraging General Franco in Spain in the 1930's. If he is regarded as deserting Garibaldi at the end of 1860 he is open to the charge of betraying the ardour and bravery of thousands of simple men in the interests of his own narrow dynastic aims and his own narrowly based political party. And the end of it is a sorry picture of half Italy governed against its will on the only flimsily legal basis of plebiscites as unreliable as those of Napoleon III and Hitler. It is true that all these ugly facts were glossed over or explained away and that Cavour was forgiven everything and treated as a hero. To persist in applauding him as a man who sought and successfully achieved Italian unity no matter what the cost, was to reflect the fact that it was his political allies who won in

Italy, and who were therefore in a position to create a myth in which he was the supreme hero. It also reflects the fact that his activities were seen in the England of his day as a praiseworthy triumph over the Whigs' two chief bogey-men, Napoleon III and Pius IX. A less trivial view is that the conventional interpretation of the facts of the years 1858–61 justifies the charge that Cavour was the first of the many who have used a claim to be acting in the interests of a nation's sacred egoism as if it were a sufficient excuse for every sort of unscrupulousness in politics. The long failure of historians to apply normal standards of morality to what they understood to be Cavour's conduct is quite shocking. When Queen Victoria, with a clairvoyant common sense that infuriated Lord John Russell, said that Sardinian activities in Naples were 'morally bad and reprehensible in themselves' Lord John could reply only by talking irrelevant twaddle about William of Orange. The Queen, like everybody else, was mistaken about Cavour; but her comment came a good deal nearer to a right judgment than the verdicts either of the three wise men of her Cabinet or of those later historians who forgave Cavour everything in much the same way as the German liberals forgave Bismarck everything, merely because he appeared to have been successful.

It is therefore important to realize that, ambitious and unscrupulous though Cavour was, his original purpose was a limited one, and that whatever views may be taken of his methods up to April 1860 (and they are certainly questionable) his conduct thereafter represents a series of reactions, at first hesitant and then cool and skilful, to a situation thrust on him by Garibaldi. In this second phase, Cavour seems at first sight more sinister than in the first. Up to April 1860 he is concerned with outmanœuvring the Austrians and their hangers-on and with managing Napoleon III; and his victims in this period of his work do not perhaps deserve a great deal of sympathy. Throughout 1860, however, he was outmanœuvring Garibaldi and a considerable section of the Italian people, and doing so in a manner singularly devoid either of generosity or honesty. At first sight, one is struck by Cavour's narrowness of vision, by the indecent haste with which he sought to discredit Garibaldi and to stifle the ardour of the Radicals who had achieved by dash and bravery successes he had been too cautious even to contemplate. (Thus, the Piedmontese army, when it advanced through the Papal States towards Naples in 1860 had not even any maps of the area.) Yet, at a deeper level, Cavour was perhaps less wrong than Garibaldi. The core of Cavour's policy was not unification but freedom from Austria, coupled with the development under Piedmontese sovereignty of free institutions in those parts of Italy which were fitted for them, and which could, with the minimum of risk (though still a high risk) be assimilated by Piedmont. Garibaldi, however, like Mazzini had no rational political aims at all, except liberty and unity as such. True, Mazzini saw the achievement of nationhood as a prelude to the regeneration of the whole European society under the principles of Humanity, but this was mere mysticism; and while mysticism has an essential place in religion it has none in politics, except perhaps the dangerous function of filling people's minds with hopes that are incapable of fulfilment. And although Garibaldi had, by 1860, so far parted company with Mazzini as to believe that nationality and humanity could be served by putting all Italy under the flag of Victor Emmanuel, the fact was that he was fundamentally as empty of constructive political purpose as Mazzini, and even less clear-sighted. For even Mazzini was not fool enough to suppose that the regeneration of Europe, or Italy, or anywhere under the sun, could be achieved under the aegis of Victor Emmanuel, of all people. It is easy to blame Cavour for wanting a swift annexation of the South to Piedmont, with no questions asked, with Rome saved, the Radical revolutionaries sent packing and Garibaldi treated like discarded orange peel. Yet Garibaldi also wanted the South to go to Victor Emmanuel. His only objections were not the sensible ones that the South did not want annexation in the form they were going to get it or that Piedmont would govern harshly. What he was sorry about was solely that he had not been allowed to go on to make still further attacks on the outraged dignity of the Pope and on the equally outraged law of Europe by taking Rome and Venetia. Cavour used a great deal of sharp practice in dealing with Garibaldi in 1860; but it must not be overlooked that Garibaldi's policy was simply war unlimited, and that it was far better for Italy that he was stopped by other Italians and in Italy, and not by the inevitable European intervention that might have put all in jeopardy, and perhaps have made of Italy another such place as Hungary had become since 1849.

Thus the truth about Cavour is not that he dared all for the national ideal, never once stopping until the dream of a united Italy had been fulfilled. Cavour did not think national unity an aim that justified the contemptuous violation of all the normal rules of political and international conduct. His career does not, as it has so often seemed to, provide a precedent and an example of the notion that an appeal to the principle of nationality makes war, double-dealing and the fomentation of plots within the territories of other governments somehow highly creditable actions which ought to be applauded. Like Bismarck after him, Cavour was both an anti-revolutionary and an anti-nationalist. He saw clearly that in practice the gospel of nationality meant war without end. He was slower than Napoleon III to see it, for Napoleon realized it after Magenta and Solferino; but in the end the outstanding work of Cavour as an Italian statesman was not to achieve Italian unification in 1860, but to prevent it. That Rome and Venetia were not within the Kingdom of Italy in 1861, in flat contradiction to the declared aims of Garibaldi and the Radicals, but that what had been gained was safe from all chance of foreign interference: these are the facts on which Cavour's claim to greatness rests. And facts very like them are the basis of Bismarck's greatness also.

XI

BISMARCK AND GERMANY 1862–1871

BECAUSE the events of the sixties with which Bismarck is connected are so familiar it is usual to suppose that they are relatively easy to understand. Yet the two commonest interpretations of those events ought to have been abandoned long ago.

The first of these is the interpretation 'Bismarck unified Germany'. He did not. He did not even want to. He annexed, conquered or absorbed into Prussian control all the states of the old German Confederation except Austria, added thereto Slesvig, Alsace and Lorraine and called the result 'The German Empire'. It was *a* German Empire, certainly; but it was not, and Bismarck never intended it to be, *the* German Empire. It excluded, deliberately, all the Germans living within the Habsburg territories of Austria and Bohemia. Thus Bismarck's German Empire was based on the division of Germany, not its unification. The Kaiser's Reich was *a* German Empire; it was Hitler's Reich that was *the* German Empire. This is the real sense in which Bismarck was a man with a limited objective.

The second interpretation which should be abandoned is that Bismarck planned the events of the sixties in advance, and that when he planned them the results were always what he had intended. We are often asked to believe that his master plan for the sixties was as follows:

1. To secure Russian neutrality: this was cleverly done by assisting them in the Polish affair of 1863.

2. To make war with Denmark in 1864 in alliance with Austria, for the purpose of having a war with Austria on this issue in 1866.
3. To secure Napoleon III's benevolent neutrality in the war with Austria by deceiving him at Biarritz into thinking he would get compensations for France when the war was over.
4. To defeat Austria in 1866, but to take no territory from her because he wanted her friendship in the coming war with France.
5. To engineer the Hohenzollern candidature in Spain in order to provoke France into declaring war in 1870.

This view of Bismarck as the dynamic ruthless realist planning the whole of this campaign brilliantly and wickedly in advance is based not on the facts but on a legend; a legend created by Bismarck to minister to his own vanity as an individual and to the cause of his indispensability as a politician. The legend was created while the events were in progress and cast into permanent form in his Memoirs, whose chief purpose was to prove that all his predecessors and all his successors were fools, that he alone was the Man, and that wisdom had been born in Germany with his accession to power in 1862, and had died with his dismissal in 1890.

The legend was assisted by Bismarck's obvious gift for the striking phrase and the memorable anecdote. The sayings of Bismarck that have passed into the currency of historical writing about the period have a freshness and directness about them that make him the century's most quotable statesman. But the bluntness was nearly always calculated, and the good story nearly always told with an immediate and precise political purpose. The sayings of Bismarck were uttered not because they were true but because they were what he wanted his hearers to believe was true.

Thus when he became Minister President in Prussia he volunteered the information that he would be like a Strafford to the King of Prussia. This was the precise opposite of what he intended to be. William of Prussia was no Charles I and the Prussian Parliament had no Pym. Strafford died, thrown over by a weak and helpless king in the grip of a fierce caucus driving towards the capture of supreme power. Bismarck had no intention of dying, and nobody had any intention of killing him. But talk about Strafford struck the right dramatic note and, lost in admiration of it, writers lose also their sense of historical accuracy when referring to it.

Like considerations apply to his famous observation about blood and iron. As an exercise in effective literary antithesis it is superb; not votes and debates, but blood and iron. But to jump from admiration of the phrase to the conclusion that it adequately describes Bismarck's methods is to forget that he said it as part of a vigorous political speech condemning the opposition of the Prussian Liberals to the increased army estimates. It is also to commit a major error of historical interpretation. From a technical point of view the distinctive achievement of Bismarck is that few statesmen in modern history have achieved such a revolution in the balance of forces in Europe with such an economy of blood and iron. The military successes of Prussia from 1864 to 1871 were brought about under the leadership of a civilian minded minister who, like Clemenceau, believed that war was too serious a business to be left to the soldiers. Bismarck did not have two characters, a warlike aggressive one before 1871 and a peaceful defensive one after 1871. He had a cautious, calculating preference for limited objectives from start to finish. He used the army when it became impossible to achieve his diplomatic purposes without it; when diplomacy alone would suffice, he merely used the army as a modern headmaster is supposed to use the cane in his study—as a threat.

The notion that all Bismarck's predecessors were incompetent fools is another of Bismarck's exaggerations. They faced extreme risks in any attempt to assert Prussian predominance in Germany. First, there was the existence of the Holy Alliance, to whose principles Nicholas I rigidly adhered in German affairs. To attempt to push Prussian claims against Austria by means of war at any time before 1853 would have meant a war against Russia as well. This is shown by the persistent opposition of Nicholas to the various schemes of Frederick William IV and his advisers between 1848 and 1851. Second, there was the situation in Germany itself. To fight Austria would be to espouse the cause of German Liberalism in the eyes, not only of the Czar, but also of German Liberals: and Prussia could not see how to fight a revolutionary war without being revolutionized herself. Prussia's position was the reverse of that of Piedmont in Italy. Piedmont's army was the creation of Liberalism. Prussia's army was the enemy of Liberalism, was the dominant social force in the state, and accepted the Liberal constitution of 1848 as grudgingly and as insincerely as the German army accepted the Weimar Constitution after 1919. In short, before 1853, a Prussian attempt to dominate even northern Germany would have involved a war against Austria, against Russia and against the Germans. Prussia declined the risk; for the avoidance of risk had been the historic tradition of Prussian policy from the days of the Great Elector onwards.

When Bismarck assumed power in Prussia in 1861, the problem of how to avoid war with Russia as the defender of the Holy Alliance had been solved for him. The Crimean War had isolated Austria from Russia and had greatly weakened Russia, perhaps more than Bismarck realized. The emergence of Napoleon III had, by the Italian affair, further undermined the old order in Europe. In terms of relative strengths, Prussia was in a far sounder position in 1861 than at any time since 1815. Concerted action against Bismarck was also out of the question. England was on bad terms with France, Russia and Austria. Russia was on bad terms with England and Austria. Napoleon III and Russia were on good terms with each other but on bad terms with everybody else: and both were concerned to change, not to maintain, the European system as it existed in 1862; Napoleon III was still in favour of destroying what was left of the 1815 Settlement and Alexander II was solely concerned with destroying the Peace of Paris.

Thus, when Bismarck came to power, the dominant factor in the European situation was the Franco-Russian *entente* which Napoleon III had created in 1856. The strength of this *entente* appeared greater than it was because of the absence of any other combination to balance it. The obvious thing for Bismarck to do, it seemed, was to make a third to this essentially anti-Austrian *entente*. Then, when putting pressure on Austria, he could rely on simultaneous pressure being applied by France, in the interests of getting Venetia for the Italians, and by Russia, in the interests of restoring her authority in the Balkans and the Black Sea, and perhaps get what he wanted without fighting for it. It is difficult to see how, faced with such a combination, even the Austrians could have been insane enough to issue one of their fatuous ultimatums.

The Polish affair of 1863 was therefore loss rather than gain for Bismarck because it broke the Franco-Russian *entente* and thus made it more difficult to work in conjunction with these two Powers. Bismarck's offer to assist Russia against the Poles in that year was not a brilliantly successful device for substituting Prussia for France as Russia's ally. It appeared to the Russians that whereas the other European powers were being straightforward nuisances over the matter, the Prussians were cunningly trying to make capital out of Russian difficulties in Poland, just as they had tried to make capital out of

Austria's difficulties in Italy in 1859. The persistent hostility with which Bismarck was viewed by the Russian Chancellor Gorchakov dates from Bismarck's officious interference in the Polish affair. That Russia did not act against Prussia in the sixties was due chiefly to her weakness after the Crimean War, her consequent close concentration on the one issue of the Black Sea clauses, and to her mistrust of Austria. Only by a close alliance with Austria could Bismarck ever again upset the Russians, as the events of 1878–1879 clearly show.

Incidentally, if Bismarck had been merely a man of blood and iron, he could have had a war against France and Austria in 1863. The immediate consequence of the Alvensleben Convention with Russia about the Poles was a Russian suggestion for an immediate Prusso-Russian war against France and Austria. Faced with the full implications of what he had done in this matter of the Poles, Bismarck backed away; a further confirmation in the eyes of the Russians of what seemed the insincerity of Prussian intentions. For his part, Bismarck was obviously not going to fight a war whose purpose would be Russian and which would have turned all Germany against him; but here again is proof that the Alvensleben Convention was an embarrassing blunder rather than a stroke of genius.

Bismarck's position was now unhappy in the extreme. The collapse of the Franco-Russian *entente* because of the Polish affair meant that he could not now hope to use their combined assistance against Austria; with that assistance he might have got at least control of northern Germany without a war at all. Worse still, the Austrians were now tiresomely masquerading as a Liberal power. Since 1861 Austria had a German Parliament, whereas Bismarck had made himself the declared enemy of Liberalism by masquerading as Strafford. Thus emboldened, Austria proposed, at an Assembly of Princes in Frankfurt in 1863, a reform of the Confederation, one feature of which would be the creation of an assembly of delegates from the various Parliaments. The Bismarckian reply stated quite clearly, however, the character of the conjuring trick he was eventually to perform. The Austrian proposals were rejected by Prussia, first because they did not provide for Prussia's absolute equality with Austria; and second because Prussia would yield none of her rights except to a Parliament 'representing the whole German nation'. Somehow, Bismarck was going to combine the full maintenance of the rights of Prussia with the existence of a Parliament representing 'the whole German nation'. In 1863 it is doubtful if anybody believed Bismarck capable of fostering a Parliament representing the whole German nation: and presumably he put the idea on paper merely as a counter to Austria's equally fraudulent Liberalism.

When the Slesvig-Holstein affair arose again, Bismarck intervened because he had to. All German opinion demanded action; but what Bismarck did was proof that he used the cant phrases of the mid-nineteenth century chiefly to deceive. The last thing he intended was to act in the Duchies for the greater glory of Germans or of the German Confederation. To act as the leader of German National and Liberal policy on this issue was certain to involve a further breach with Austria, but a breach in which he would have had to act as Prussia had been intended to act in Denmark in 1848. This was precisely what he had every intention of not doing. He therefore entered into alliance with Austria in order to protect himself from the Germans rather than as a cunning preliminary to a war with Austria two years later.

A careful look at the details of what went on over Slesvig-Holstein shows that if Bismarck's aim in 1864 really was war with Austria then his behaviour is an outstanding example of a diplomat performing the feat of going to Birmingham by way of Beachy Head. It is clear only that Bismarck wanted the question settled in the interests of Prussia, and not in the interests of the German Confederation. To assist him in this aim, he made his alliance with Austria. Austria accepted the alliance because Austria likewise did not want either to exalt the secondary states, or to allow Prussia to take control of the problem. Having defeated the aims of the Confederation by the end of the war, when the Duchies passed into Austro-Prussian hands (instead of those of Augustenberg, the Confederation's candidate) both sides proceeded to haggle over what was to happen next. Austria was hampered by a fundamental lack of interest in the Duchies and by her fear that if she made too many difficulties there would be trouble in Hungary and Venetia. Hence Austria proposed that in return for her agreement to a Prussian annexation of the Duchies, Bismarck should cede part of Silesia to Austria and guarantee Austria's position in Italy and Hungary. Given that Bismarck had himself offered to guarantee Venetia in return for the Prussian acquisition of the Duchies it is difficult to see much sense in the exorbitance of Austria's demands.

Bismarck still did not explode any war against Austria. He 'papered over the cracks' at Gastein twelve months later in August 1865. There can be only two reasons why Bismarck still held his hand. First he was afraid of the Germans. Throughout Germany, the annexation of the Duchies had made Prussia detested. So far from leading Germany, Bismarck was earning its hatred. How then could he fight a war with Austria even as a fraudulent leader of German feeling? Given the anti-Prussian sentiment that prevailed, the fraud would deceive nobody. The second reason for delay was that he was afraid of Napoleon III.

The story goes that Bismarck had seen through Napoleon III. Since everybody who has written any history at all since 1871 also claims to have seen through Napoleon III, it is inevitable that the story should be regarded as true. Yet for a man of blood and iron faced with the task of dealing with an obvious charlatan, Bismarck acted with such extraordinary caution that it is only to be explained by abandoning the whole theory. Bismarck had not yet seen through Napoleon III; and anyway he was much too clever to believe in other people's appearance of folly. The facts of the relations between the two men seem very un-melodramatic. Bismarck was on good terms with Napoleon III and wanted to make sure of his support. He also wanted to find out what price Napoleon III would demand for that support.

The rebuff Napoleon III had received from Russia over Poland, coupled with his determination somehow to get Venetia for Italy without having to fight the Austrians again, made him anxious to keep on good terms with the Prussians. He had not been prepared to fight against them for the defence of Denmark. The French army was in no condition to fight. The English were in no condition to help him. His mind was already on Mexico. The principle of nationality inclined him to side with the Germans against the Danes. If he antagonized Prussia he would lose his last European friend. In other words, Bismarck did not create or deceive the French into a Franco-Prussian alliance. Circumstances had made it for him.

Napoleon III must have found Bismarck at Biarritz quite a pleasant change after Cavour at Plombières. Bismarck did not want Napoleon III to do anything, and this in itself must have been satisfactory. To sit still while Bismarck excluded Austria from northern Germany was a quite acceptable programme to Napoleon. As for what he himself might get out of it, he evidently refused to commit himself. He had made a bad mistake at Plombières by committing himself in advance of the event and he was not going to make the mistake a second time. He contented himself therefore with expressing his anxiety to see Venetia handed over to the Italians.

Thus Bismarck did not deceive Napoleon III at Biarritz.

Napoleon III tried to deceive Bismarck. Bismarck was to plunge into an uncertain adventure not knowing how big a share of the spoils Napoleon would demand, nor when he would demand it. One of the stories Bismarck tells which seems to fit the facts is his assertion that when Benedetti came to him immediately after Sadowa he hardly dared to breathe so great was his fear of what the Frenchman might have been sent to demand of him.

Thus Bismarck learned from going to Biarritz little more than he would have done by staying at Berlin. He had to go on, conscious all the time he manœuvred against the Austrians that he was gambling on being in a position to pay Napoleon's unnamed price whenever the latter presented his bill. However, Bismarck kept his side of the bargain, by the agreement with Italy in 1866. To this Napoleon gave his paternal blessing, because it assured in the event of a Prussian victory that Napoleon's only concrete aim would be achieved.

The Prusso-Italian treaty made it almost certain that Austria would fight, by making it impossible for her to strike a bargain. Before it, it was still possible for Austria to make an agreement with Prussia over the Duchies on the basis of a Prussian promise to defend Austria in Venetia. But, to please Napoleon III, Bismarck had blocked that line of escape. Indeed, Austria's reaction to the Prusso-Italian treaty was an attempt not to bargain the Prussians out of it, but the Italians. They could have Venetia, they were told. The offer to Italy implied a decision not to bargain any more with the Prussians.

If the treaty with Italy made sure of French neutrality, there was still the more intractable problem of the Germans. The attempt to solve the problem was yet another project, issued by Prussia the day after the signature of the treaty with Italy, for the reform of the German Confederation. A National Assembly was to be elected, on the basis of universal suffrage, and the Austrians were to be excluded from the new Germany. Once again, the offer was treated by Germany with indifference. It was absurd to suppose that reactionary Prussia could seriously intend a Germany based on universal suffrage, for universal suffrage was an extremist demand. If Bismarck was at odds with the Liberals, it was ridiculous to suppose that he seriously meant to accept the Radical demand for universal suffrage. The consequence was that Prussia did, after all, have to fight virtually all Germany.

Bismarck suggests that he was in a state of continuous nervous anxiety throughout the Seven Weeks War; and there is every reason to believe it. Sadowa had the same relation to the Prussian attack on Austria as Solferino had to the Franco-Sardinian attack on Austria. Each was enough to make the Austrians ready for concessions, but neither was enough to make them abandon everything. But because Napoleon III had committed himself in advance to a complete expulsion of Austria from Italy his withdrawal from the war after Solferino appeared cowardly. Bismarck's withdrawal, since he had never committed himself to the complete solution of the German problem, seemed a masterpiece of diplomacy. Yet although Bismarck's withdrawal was a carefully premeditated act, it was to some extent dictated by military considerations not unlike those that governed Napoleon III's withdrawal from Italy. It was also due to Bismarck's continuing uncertainty as to what the French were going to do. The Empress Eugénie was urging Napoleon III to do to Prussia in 1866 what Prussia had done to France in 1859—mobilize. It is a fair guess that Bismarck's memory was at least as good as Eugénie's. He was completely in the dark about Napoleon III. He had failed to solve the riddle of the Sphinx at Biarritz and he had no means of knowing immediately after Sadowa that there was, as he had subsequently said, no riddle to solve. The decision to stop after Sadowa was based on a number of considerations; but the most important were those of elementary military and diplomatic precaution.

The usual suggestion is that there were two main reasons for the early cessation of war. He was not ready for a war against France. Therefore he would not provoke her by continuing the attack on Austria to the point where Austria would agree to the unification of all Germany under Prussia. Second, he did not want to humiliate Austria since he wished her to be neutral in the war with France when it eventually came.

The notion that Austria would be neutral in a Franco-Prussian war *because* Prussia had taken no territory from her after Sadowa does seem to suggest a view of the Austrian intelligence too insulting to be just even to them. The Austrians and Napoleon III were actually in treaty relations with each other in 1866. The Austrians had fought with France against Prussia in the Seven Years War and might do so again. The French belief in 1870 that Austria would join them against Prussia was mistaken but not based entirely on imagination. If Bismarck had in fact secured Austrian neutrality in 1870 by his tactics in 1866 it is surprising that hardly anybody in Paris and not even everybody in Vienna seems to have realized it. The neutrality of Austria in 1870, like the neutrality of Russia in 1866, was not in fact conjured out of nothing by Bismarck. Both were the data of his diplomatic geometry; neither was a problem given him to solve. Austrian intervention on the side of France, though not impossible, was highly improbable before the Franco-Prussian war started and out of the question once it had.

As for the effect of 1866 on Napoleon III, the quick Prussian victory was certainly a disappointment but when it came to doing something about it, he decided as so often in favour of doing nothing. He made no demands on Bismarck before agreeing to the peace terms; and cancelled mobiliza-

GERMAN BOUNDARIES
1815 - 71
SLESVIG
HOLSTEIN
THE MECKLENBURGS
OLDENBERG
HANOVER
NETHERLANDS
WESTPHALIA
P R U S S I A
BELGIUM
HESSE
NASSAU
THURINGIA
SAXONY
SILESIA
BOHEMIA
MORAVIA
LORRAINE
ALSACE
BADEN
WURTEMBERG
BAVARIA
LOWER AUSTRIA
UPPER AUSTRIA
FRANCE
SWITZERLAND
SALZBURG
STYRIA
TYROL
CARINTHIA
SAVOY
KINGDOM OF SARDINIA
LOMBARDY
VENETIA
The German Confederation 1815
Prussia in 1864
Territory annexed by Prussia, 1866-7
North German Confederation, 1866
German Empire, 1871

tion orders shortly after issuing them. No doubt the decision to do nothing was a turning point in the history of France and Germany and indeed of all Europe. But Napoleon III did not think so.

What now looks like a colossal error seemed, in the light of the international situation in 1866, a quite reasonable policy. The setting up of the North German Confederation under Prussian control could be defended on the grounds of common sense and of national principle, and from the point of view of international peace and the balance of power. A tiresome international problem, that of a continuous struggle between Austria and Prussia for control over an irrationally large number of separate sovereignties, had been speedily settled in a way that provided a proper Prussian balance to the power of Austria, which hitherto had been far in excess either of its deserts or its real political usefulness. By making the division of Germany more rational, the Peace of Prague might even be said to have made the division look more permanent. By making the south German states independent of Austria it made them potential allies of France, their only possible protector against Prussia, to whom they were traditionally hostile. Finally, the peace could properly be regarded as having strengthened Prussia, the ally of France and Russia, against Austria, the enemy of all three.

There was thus no particular reason why Napoleon III should either mobilize against Prussia or demand compensations. France appeared to have benefited by the Peace of Prague. From Napoleon III's personal point of view it solved the vexed question of Venetia: and it appeared to have liberated Germany without imposing on her the sort of unity that Cavour had imposed on Italy. Italian unity contradicted history. The North German Confederation, by leaving the Catholic South independent, did not. In short, the Peace of Prague achieved in Germany exactly the sort of solution acceptable to France that the Peace of Zurich had intended to provide in Italy.

The demand for compensation, to which Napoleon III yielded, immediately after it was too late to make the demand effectively, was the outcry of hurt French vanity, of military jealousy, of Catholic pique, and of popular xenophobia skilfully worked up by opposition politicians as a means of discrediting the Emperor. Had Napoleon III kept out of Mexico; had his physical strength been unimpaired; had he not been compelled by past errors and present weakness to make concessions to the so-called Liberal opposition; had there been no Liberal Empire in 1870; had the Press been muzzled in the late sixties as it had been in the fifties; in short, had Napoleon III been absolute ruler of France between 1866 and 1870; then there would have been less of that vacillating and undignified search for compensations in the Rhineland, or Luxembourg or Belgium, less of the senseless exhibitionism which disgraced French politicians in 1870 and afflicted them with the madness of those whom the gods wish to destroy. Any assessment of responsibility for the Franco-Prussian war that places the burden exclusively on either Napoleon III or Bismarck is inadequate. The other guilty parties clearly include those who led the French Opposition, those who pandered to it—Gramont and Ollivier—and those around the Emperor—Eugénie and Rouher—who bullied him into spineless, tearful acceptance of their frantic notion that a war would save him. Responsibility needs to be borne also by the French high command for their conceit and ignorance. (If the French army was so much better than the Prussians what good reason was there for being scared by Prussian gains in 1866?) Responsible also were the French middle class who asked for a war while declining to pay the cost of military re-organization and refusing to regard conscription as proper for anybody but the workers and peasants.

In these last tragic years Napoleon III was swept aside as completely by the French as a decade before he had been swept aside by the Italians. The way in which the compensation proposals were so conspicuously bungled shows in itself how little they reflected a clearly directed policy. They made nonsense of Napoleon's claim to be the protector of the nations, and show that he had lost his nerve and his strength and was pursuing in despair and confusion a policy that was not his own and which he knew he could not sustain by an appeal to force. Of course, as a congenital conspirator he wanted to get what he could out of the changed situation. But once the fighting in Bohemia had stopped, it was too late. Worse still, as the various French moves were made, Bismarck took appropriate steps to insure himself against the aggressive state of mind they indicated. He was not now, any more than at Biarritz, luring Napoleon III to destruction. The French were doing the job for him.

The usual assumption is that in sponsoring the Hohenzollern candidature in Spain Bismarck was planning to provoke France into war. It is however important to realize that there are three distinct phases in the story of the Hohenzollern candidature, and that the two latter phases could not have been foreseen by Bismarck when he first launched the scheme.

The plan, as originally devised, was to get Leopold selected as King of Spain before anybody suspected that he was being put forward as a serious candidate. What Bismarck's precise purpose was in pushing forward the candidature in face of the reluctance of the Hohenzollerns and the strong opposition of the King of Prussia will never be known, since the plan failed to come into operation. The view that Bismarck expected the selection of a Hohenzollern prince as King of Spain to provoke Napoleon III into war appears to be based partly on the fact that Bismarck subsequently said that that was his intention. This is of course not evidence at all. Since the war ended in victory and in the proclamation of the German Empire, Bismarck would automatically claim to have planned the whole thing from start to finish. The only other evidence is not much more reliable. It appears to consist of opinions expressed as to his intentions by some of his associates. There are however two matters about which it is usually almost impossible to be certain at any time. One is the precise intentions of Bismarck in initiating any particular plan; and the other is the likely reaction of Napoleon III to any particular situation, especially after 1866. Bismarck was far too supple and Napoleon III far too muddled and helpless. Therefore evidence is lacking as to Bismarck's real intention in engineering the candidature; and he cannot have felt completely certain as to how Napoleon III would react to the *fait accompli* with which it was hoped to face him. Obviously, Napoleon would greatly resent the consequent exaltation of the Hohenzollern dynasty, and by the shabbiest means, at the expense of the prestige and security of his own position. It is true also, that the possibility of a war with France was always present in Bismarck's mind, if only because there were few possibilities that were not present in it. But to say anything more definite than this about Bismarck's reasons for his scheme is to make assertions which appear unverifiable.

The second phase of the story begins when, contrary to Bismarck's intentions, the fact of the candidature became public before Leopold could be formally chosen king. None of the developments which took place from this time on could have been foreseen by Bismarck because he had not in fact intended them. Instead of a situation in which France reacted to a *fait accompli*, he faced one in which France was reacting to a mere proposal. There is a strong suspicion that in this second phase, Bismarck, having seen that the whole thing had misfired, behaved as if he had nothing to do with it solely because it had misfired, and not because he was trying to maintain an appearance of innocence—which nobody in Europe believed anyway. One thing was certain: with Bismarck away in Pomerania, and the matter being handled at Ems by the King, the end of it was bound to be the withdrawal of the candidature, since that was the sole aim the King had in mind. This would present the world with the unusual spectacle of the French scoring a resounding diplomatic triumph at the expense of the Prussians: a triumph, also, in which European opinion was on the whole favourable to the French. Bismarck in fact made no move to go to Ems until he had received news that the matter was closed.

The third phase, again quite unpredictable in advance, opens with the presentation by Benedetti of the *à tout jamais* demand and was ended swiftly by Bismarck's publication of the manipulated Ems telegram. Only out of this last phase does a specific 'cause' of war emerge at all; and only at this stage is it absolutely certain that Bismarck was provoking war. For, thanks to the courteous moderation of the King of Prussia, peace was still certain until the carefully publicized despatch of the Ems telegram. The action of Bismarck was his own free choice and he must bear responsibility. Faced with the convincing evidence of the virulent anti-Germanism of the French; faced with the superb opportunity now presented to him of making a war for the aggrandisement of Prussia look like a war of national defence against French hostility; faced with the choice between continuing to acquiesce, for the first time, in a public humiliation of Prussia or of transforming humiliation into a once-and-for-all triumph, he took the only course such a man might be expected to take. The readiness to make war on France if necessary had doubtless been there since 1866; but the decision to have the war in 1870 was made in 1870, and after the affair of the Hohenzollern Candidature had ended.

Yet, like most successful conquerors, Bismarck could have done but little had not his victims made themselves his accomplices by their folly. Not content with making the *à tout jamais* demand, the French committed the additional folly of declaring war without bothering about Benedetti's own version of the Ems incident. Nothing is more frightening than the contrast between the dreadful and irrevocable consequences of this war and the triviality and irrationality of those on both sides who made it. It was a war entirely without intelligible causes. France had nothing to gain from victory except to perpetuate and deepen German disunity on terms to which Germans could never be reconciled. Bismarck had few valid reasons either. He did not go to war to get Alsace-Lorraine or to overthrow Napoleon III, and both results of the war were bad for Germany. Only Napoleon III stood between the Germans and the hysterical pride of the French who were attacking the Emperor because, in the words of Thiers, he acted in the interests of Italians, Germans and Poles but never in the interests of France. A France that repudiated Napoleon III because he had lost a war might too easily become a France bent on one day reversing the verdict of that war. A France deprived of Alsace-Lorraine by war guaranteed the insecurity of Germany.

Nor did Bismarck necessarily have to go to war to 'unite' Germany in the sense of getting the South German States into a German Empire. In all but name that unification was complete in both military and economic affairs before 1870. The practical differences between the fundamental structure of Germany after 1866 and its structure after 1871 were altogether too small to be worth a large-scale war. As for satisfying German national aspirations, Bismarck never became the instrument of these. He made war therefore for reasons as criminally irrational as those which influenced the French. To avoid a setback to Prussian influence and prestige, and to himself, he deliberately aroused the mass emotions of the Germans and incited those of the French and impelled both peoples into a war which inflicted on European society wounds so deep that they have never since been healed. It is melancholy therefore to observe that Dr Eyck, the latest of Bismarck's biographers, can nevertheless speak of the creation of the German Empire by means of this war as proof of Bismarck's 'singular greatness' and 'everlasting glory'.

In considering Bismarck's aims and methods in Germany it has long been customary to compare him with Cavour; and it is certainly instructive to realize that they both sought to limit the Nationalism they claimed to be fulfilling. Yet it is perhaps even more illuminating to compare him with Napoleon III. The constitution of the German Empire was much the same sort of transparent confidence trick as the constitution of the Second Empire in 1852. There was first the lie involved in the word 'Empire'. Both France after 1852 and Germany after 1871 were called Empires to disguise the fact that they were not Empires. The Second Empire did not give France back her control of all Western Europe and the Bismarckian Empire did not give William I an Empire over all the Germans. The Second French Empire was nothing like the First French Empire. It was very little bigger than the French kingdom under the Bourbons or under Louis Philippe. In the same way to describe as 'the German Empire' a region which excluded of deliberate purpose all the Germans of Austria and Bohemia was just the sort of falsehood that Hitler might have had in mind when he said that the bigger a lie was the more likely people were to believe it. From 1871 to 1914 all the world's atlases solemnly described as 'The German Empire' what was in reality a Prussian Empire; and all the world's history books have gone on gravely describing as the 'unification' of Germany what was in reality the division of it.

The unification of Germany was the one thing Bismarck

was determined to prevent, because his whole purpose was the preservation of Prussian power against the rising tide of Liberalism and Radicalism. The demand for real German unity had been made clearly enough in 1848: but by the revolutionaries, and that in itself was enough to damn it. Bismarck was therefore fighting both Liberals and Radicals in Germany between 1862 and 1871, just as Napoleon III fought the same forces in France between 1848 and 1851. From 1862 till just after Sadowa the Liberals were opposed to him because he was acting in defiance of the Prussian Constitution. But just as, beneath the surface, the Liberals in the Second Republic wanted Louis Napoleon as their ally against the Reds, so in Prussia the Liberals wanted Bismarck as their ally against the rest of Germany. Many French Liberals forgave Louis Napoleon the *coup d'état* in the interests of internal security. Most Prussian Liberals forgave Bismarck his illegal collection of taxes from 1862 to 1866 because he had created the North German Confederation, and won a decisive military victory for Prussia.

It was probably much to his surprise that Bismarck found victory over the Liberals so easy. No police action was necessary against them, as it had been in France. Prussian Liberalism surrendered after Sadowa as completely as the Austrians. Its reward was that by the Imperial Constitution of 1871 Bismarck treated parliamentary Liberalism with the contempt the Liberals had themselves shown for it. When he graciously condescended after Sadowa to ask them to indemnify him for having collected taxes for four years in defiance of the constitution, they gave him what he wanted. The implication was clear: they would forgive absolutism and militarism if they achieved military glory. Consequently, although on paper Bismarck's Imperial Reichstag had more power than Napoleon III's Legislative Assembly, it had very little more. Its budgetary control was hardly greater; it was equally powerless to initiate legislation. It had no more control over the effective head of the state (the Imperial Chancellor) than the French Chamber had over Napoleon III. The Bundesrat was as empty a substitute for an upper chamber as Napoleon III's Senate. The various Imperial Ministers or Secretaries of State were as much the agents of Bismarck as the Ministers of Napoleon III were mere 'aids to the Imperial intelligence'.

In dealing with the Radicals, both Bismarck and Napoleon III realized that it was possible to do a political conjuring trick with universal suffrage, too. The Radicals, generalizing from their views of the urban proletariat and their equally town-bred intellectual leaders, assumed that the enfranchisement of the masses was a short cut to revolution. This was one of the sadder and sillier mistakes of the extremists of 1848. The event proved that universal suffrage returned Right Wing deputies to the Assembly of the Second Republic, and made Louis Napoleon President. For the masses were not urban in the mid-nineteenth century; they were peasants. The success of Napoleon III had proved beyond doubt that universal suffrage, so far from being dangerous to Conservatism or to dictatorship, was its willing ally. By means of it, first Napoleon III and then Bismarck could claim to be appealing to 'the people' over the heads of the bourgeois politicians, and thus masquerade as autocrats who were also revolutionaries. The fact that the formal constitution condemned the bourgeois politicians to futility suited the masses just as much as it suited the absolute ruler. To the masses (i.e. the peasants) Liberal and Radical politics were either meaningless, or else a means of ensuring that the state machine was operated in the interests of the professional classes, the town workers, and the landlords.

The constitutions of the Second Empire and of the Second Reich alike fooled the Liberals with a fraudulent Parliament

CENTRAL & SOUTH - EASTERN EUROPE, 1871
Heligoland (Br.)
GERMAN EMPIRE
Berlin
Oder
Rhine
Vistula
Warsaw
POLAND
RUSSIA
Dnieper
Dniester
Pruth
AUSTRIA-HUNGARY
Vienna
Theiss
Drave
Belgrade
LORRAINE
ALSACE
FRANCE
SWITZERLAND
Venice
Florence
ITALY
Rome
RUMANIA
Bucharest
Danube
BESSARABIA
DOBRUDJA
Constantinople
BOSNIA
SERBIA
BULGARIA
Sofia
Novibazar
MONTE-NEGRO
OTTOMAN EMPIRE
GREECE

and the Radicals by the grant of universal suffrage. Both systems were systems of political fraud, the one to maintain Napoleon III and his gang in power, the other to keep Bismarck and the Prussian Army in power. Whereas Cavour made himself the champion of Liberalism and worked with the Liberals against the Radical Republicans, Bismarck, like Napoleon III, worked against both. However unscrupulously Cavour may have operated on public opinion in Italy, his appeal was primarily to the feeling for freedom. In the making of the Bismarckian Empire the appeal was to power. In consequence, Italian parliamentary life was irresponsible and factious, but it was real. German parliamentary life was irresponsible and factious also; but it was unreal as well because German politicians had no power themselves but had willed it all to the state machine. The Italian system was a poor imitation of a good model, England. The German system was a good imitation of a bad model, the Second Empire, and unlike the Constitution of 1852, Bismarck's Constitution was intended to be permanent. Cavour's methods were an unscrupulous imitation of the legitimate political activities of a free community. The National Society was an Italian version of the Anti-Corn Law League, modified to meet the tougher resistance to be overcome in Italy and backed by the armed force that an English agitation, unlike an Italian one, did not need. Bismarck's methods were those of an adventurer whose aim was to murder political liberty in its cradle, in the interests of a clique. It was the technique of the *coup d'état* of 1851 wonderfully elaborated to meet the infinitely more complicated German situation within which Bismarck had to work.

XII

BISMARCK AND GERMANY 1871–1890

IT is traditional to blame Bismarck for his wickedness up to 1871 and to praise him for his extraordinary 'diplomatic artistry' from 1871 to 1890. The praise needs as much qualification as the blame. The problems which he attempted to solve after 1871 were largely problems which he had himself brought into the realms of policy; and from the purely diplomatic point of view the particular ways in which these problems posed themselves were certainly of his making. Worse still, the story is one of failure.

Bismarck himself summed up his problem by saying that he suffered from a nightmare fear of coalitions. Contemplating the only historical precedent Prussian history provided for the situation after 1871 he found himself fearing a repetition of the situation of 1760. A powerful Prussia, which under Frederick the Great had defied all Europe at that time, was all but annihilated by a coalition of France, Austria and Russia, whose forces had for a short time occupied Berlin. His diplomacy was devoted to preventing this happening again, now that Prussia dominated Germany.

It is usual to place as much emphasis on Bismarck's policy towards France in this matter as on his policy towards Austria-Hungary and Russia. Yet France by herself was at no time a military menace to Bismarck: and most of his energy was directed towards keeping control of the problems on his eastern frontier. For the most part, Bismarck's policy towards France was conciliatory, though if everybody was convinced of the insincerity of his dealings with the French this is not to be wondered at. His essential anxiety, however, was how to prevent the problem of south-eastern Europe developing in such a way as to provide France with an ally.

He began therefore by seeking to continue the friendship with the Habsburgs and with Russia that had stood him in such good stead in 1870. He proposed a revival of the old Holy Alliance, designed to persuade the three Emperors that they had a common interest greater than their conflicting aims. It was however impossible to revive the policy of Metternich in the 1870's. The revolution in central Europe had been exorcised by Cavour and by Bismarck himself; and the republicanism against which the Emperors set their face at their meeting in 1872 could not, even by Bismarck, be worked up into a menace capable of frightening either St Petersburg or Vienna. Moreover, not only was the French problem—that of the future of Alsace-Lorraine—of his own making, but so was the east European problem, in the particular form in which he had to deal with it. His own action in 1870 had assisted the Russians to solve the problem of the Black Sea Clauses, and had thus freed them to resume a forward policy in the Balkans. Worse still, although the last thing he wanted was friction with Russia, both the creation of the German Empire and his wars against the Habsburgs had made such friction inevitable. Before 1866 the Habsburgs were a German and an Italian power. By his own war he had driven the Habsburgs out of both Germany and Italy. Therefore, if the Habsburgs were to survive as a great power at all, a 'Drive towards the east' was the only policy open to them. Yet a forward Habsburg policy in the east was incompatible with the role Bismarck wanted them somehow to fulfil. Their function, in a perfectly ordered Bismarckian world, would be that of a stable buffer-state between the Russian and German Empires in south-east Europe; and a buffer also between Bismarck and the possibility of his own Germans running him into the task of assuming responsibility for the limitless expansion of German ambitions. This would surely happen if the Habsburgs disappeared. One recalls his ferocious observations in 1866 to the generals who wanted him to march on to Vienna. Once in Vienna, he objected, you will then ask to go on to Constantinople; once in Constantinople you will want to go on and found an Empire in the east—and leave Prussia to her fate. It was as if, the day after Sadowa, he had had a vision of William II, and of Hitler, and of the catastrophe of Stalingrad. Against the full extent of German ambitions he upheld the cause of Prussia. Even when he re-christened Prussia 'The German Empire' he remained a Prussian in all his fibres. As such he behaved, whenever he could, as the instrument of a policy of purely dynastic, and never of mass or national, expansion. Perhaps after all he was the last of the Enlightened Despots, concerned exclusively with seeking a rational balance of power in an age when men's minds were increasingly turning towards megalomaniac dreams of world domination.

The clash between Austria-Hungary and Russia over the Balkan situation between 1875 and 1878 therefore demolished Bismarck's diplomatic plans for the German Empire before they had been incorporated into a single written treaty, since the Dreikaiserbund of 1872 was never precisely formulated. He was, in 1879, brought face to face with the issue he thought to have evaded: the issue of where lay the limits of German Nationalism. To say that the Eastern Question was not worth the bones of a single Pomeranian grenadier was only to say that Prussia was not interested in the Eastern Question; but the Germans were, and always had been, interested in the Eastern Question and not even Bismarck could persuade Germans to let Russia pose as the liberator of all the Slavs. Pan-Slavism did not merely menace Turkey: it menaced

Austria-Hungary equally, and therefore Germany itself. The implication of Russia's patronage of Bulgaria in 1877 was Russian control of all south-eastern Europe. True, Russia was in no desperate hurry and would not, in 1878, even go so far as to support the Serbs. Yet German acquiescence in the Bulgarian proposals of San Stefano, whether given by Bismarck or Andrassy or both, would have been an act of political suicide. Hence, Bismarck dared not be an honest broker in 1878. If he failed to maintain Austria-Hungary as a bulwark against the Russians the consequence would have to be a summons to the whole German nation to a war for the overthrow of Czardom; and given the Alsace-Lorraine problem, it would be a war on two fronts. Such a war Bismarck believed his Empire could not sustain; nor did he see how Prussian domination of that Empire could survive such a war. It would inevitably be a National war and probably a Radical war; with neither was Prussian power compatible.

Bismarck's support of Austria-Hungary at the Congress of Berlin, though it meant alienation of the Russians, was thus unavoidable. The purpose of the Dual Alliance of 1879 was to give substance, in view of Russian hostility, to his previously announced intention of being ready to resist any Russian attempt to destroy Austria-Hungary as a great power. So anxious was he to guarantee the Habsburgs that he even yielded when Andrassy refused to give him his desired *quid pro quo* of a Habsburg promise to assist Germany against France. As it stood therefore, the Dual Alliance gave the Habsburgs complete protection, since Russia was their only enemy; but it gave Germany only incomplete protection, since Austria-Hungary was not committed to assisting Germany against France. In one sense the point was academic, since Germany did not fear an attack by a France without allies: and if Russia were to join France in a war against Germany, the treaty did provide for Habsburg assistance. Yet in another sense the point was not academic. German acceptance of the task of defending Austria-Hungary was not matched by a corresponding responsibility on the part of Vienna to defend Germany; Bismarck was thus liable to find himself committed to supporting Habsburg adventures in the Balkans. By itself, therefore, the Dual Alliance did not make sense to Bismarck, since it was far more likely to provoke war than to preserve peace. What he wanted to do was to prop the Habsburg Empire up, not to harness the German army to Habsburg expansionism in the Balkans. Therefore, as well as protecting the Habsburgs against Russia, he must use Russia to protect him against the Habsburgs. This additional and essential safeguard was provided by the Three Emperors' League of 1881. By providing that Russia would not join France in a war against Germany, it seemed to dispose of his coalition nightmare. More important, it provided the necessary check on Austria-Hungary, first by the mere fact of the treaty's existence, and second by an attempt to divide the Balkans into spheres of influence. Bosnia, Herzegovina and the Sanjak were to be in the Habsburg sphere, Bulgaria and Eastern Roumelia in the Russian. It also provided against any unilateral action by Russia in the Balkans in the event of a Russo-Turkish war. The implications are clear. By the Dual Alliance, Russia must not destroy Austria-Hungary. By the Three Emperors' League Russia must not destroy Turkey, and thereby threaten the Habsburgs. But also, Austria-Hungary must not destroy Turkey either, since that would involve Bismarck in a war with Russia which he did not want. The disputed territory must be partitioned. All that diplomacy could achieve, therefore, diplomacy had done.

Unhappily, Bulgaria and Eastern Roumelia were not pieces on a chessboard and they spoiled everything by refusing to accept the passive role assigned to them. Their status could not after all be determined by diplomatic calculations, whether made by Disraeli in 1878 or by Bismarck in 1881. Bismarck could prevent poor young Alexander of Bulgaria marrying the Prussian king's grand-daughter so that Russia should have no chance of accusing Berlin of organizing another Hohenzollern candidature; but he could not prevent the Eastern Roumelian revolution from being emphatically anti-Russian in character. The result was that if Bismarck kept to the terms of the Three Emperors' League, he would find himself aligned with Russia against Austria-Hungary and England, for the sake of Russian claims on Bulgaria. By joining with England and the Habsburgs in opposing Russia's policy in Bulgaria in 1886, Bismarck in fact lost Russian friendship and did not again recover it.

The claim that the Reinsurance Treaty did achieve this feat has no substance. Signed in June 1887, it reaffirmed Bismarck's recognition of Russia's rights in Bulgaria. Before the end of August 1887 Russia was asking Bismarck to support her in ejecting Ferdinand of Saxe-Coburg from Bulgaria, and Bismarck was again failing to fulfil his obligations. So far apart had Russia and Germany become, indeed, that as his career was closing, Bismarck was toying with the idea of bringing in England to help him prop up the Habsburgs. The English were not interested: and an alliance between England and the two German powers would almost certainly have produced the war against Russia that Bismarck so anxiously wished to avoid.

Arguments as to how far the Reinsurance Treaty was incompatible with the Dual Alliance of 1879 are largely academic. The important fact about it is that it did not appreciably slow down the steady movement of Russia towards France. Indeed, by driving Russian bonds off the Berlin stock market at the end of 1887, Bismarck did as much as anybody to increase those financial links between France and Russia which preceded the closer military and diplomatic links.

Since Bismarck's worst anxieties were in the east, the adhesion, in 1882, of Italy to his alliance with the Habsburgs is of relatively minor importance. Its genesis is usually ascribed to his satanic cunning in inciting the French to annex Tunis in 1881. This was done deliberately, it is said, to make the Italians feel so annoyed, so helpless and so anti-French as to drive them instantly into his arms. It is worth recalling however that when the initiative did come from Italians, Bismarck rejected it brusquely and directed them to compose their differences with Vienna before asking him for anything. Furthermore, the advantages to Germany of Italy's membership of the Triple Alliance were on balance fewer than the advantages to Italy. The Alliance itself gave Italy protection from the Habsburgs; and its terms gave Italy protection against France without involving her in a war between the Germans and the Russians, in which Italy had no interest. With the experience of 1866 behind him, Bismarck can have been under no illusions as to the military value of an Italian alliance, and it seems unlikely that he thought it gave him against France that defence which the Habsburgs had withheld in 1879. The Triple Alliance fell in very neatly with his general scheme of things, certainly. Together with the Three Emperors' League, signed the year before, it completed the isolation of France; it eliminated the possibility of Italy embarrassing the Habsburgs by raising the matter of the Irredenta in a moment of crisis; and it pleased the English. But since by 1902 Italy had intimated that she would not allow her membership of the Triple Alliance to involve her in war with France any more than with England, the long term importance of the Triple Alliance can be exaggerated. Its signature in 1882 marks the highest point of Bismarck's influence in Europe: but by 1890 what mattered was not that the Triple Alliance still existed, but that the Three Emperors' League did not.

In the final assessment, Bismarck's outstanding achievement is to have imposed his personality on half a century of history. The state he created, and the means he devised for preserving it thereafter, were of his own unaided making. He had no collaborators; only agents, and willing and unwilling accessories. He had no spiritual or moral roots in the Europe in which he worked and triumphed. He destroyed the past, but feared the future which he built on its ruins; and for the deeper aspirations of his contemporaries he had nothing but contempt. This is perhaps most strikingly illustrated in his suggestion in 1890 that the Empire he had created should be dissolved and reconstituted without consulting anybody but the princes; and solely because he thought he could then govern it more autocratically than he was doing already. He stood, therefore, for no principles. His whole political existence was devoted to the task of putting Prussia into a position of predominance and of keeping it there, preserved inviolate against the possibility either of decline or advance. He created a Great Power and willed it not to behave like one because it would create problems he did not want to have to deal with. To give Prussia the mastery of Germany was in the end to make Prussia the agent of Germany as a power with world-wide ambitions: yet he held those ambitions in check throughout his career. Never before had the Germans possessed a state-machine capable of action against their hereditary Slav enemies. Bismarck gave them such a machine, and tried with inexhaustible ingenuity to prevent their using it for that purpose. In much the same way he created a Great Power and supposed it would not wish to assert itself by demanding oversea colonies: he yielded to the demand as if to the importunities of silly children.

Since, however, Bismarck's Reich was designed to avoid

fulfilling the aims of German Nationalism, German Liberalism, or German Radicalism, it can be more adequately described by the phrase 'a Great Power' than any other state in modern European history. It was Great and it was a Power: those were the only certainties about Bismarck's Reich. Once he was gone, therefore, German policy was devoted exclusively to the continuous assertion that Germany was powerful and great. Germany, as Bismarck manufactured it, and because of the way he manufactured it, had no other philosophy.

All else that Germany possessed was the dangerous legend he himself did so much to create, the legend of Realpolitik, and of the Lightning War. The diplomatic activities of his successors continued the tradition he himself claimed to have begun: the tradition that a ruthless 'realism' based on a studied contempt for the interests or the protests of other states was in itself a sufficient basis on which to conduct foreign relations, because in the last resort a lightning war could settle the matter once and for all.

This aspect of the Bismarckian tradition was much easier to learn than the more subtle part of it. This consisted in Bismarck's view of war as the servant of diplomacy and not its master. He understood quite clearly after 1871 that no more lightning wars were possible; he exerted much of his ingenuity before 1870 to seeking diplomatic solutions right up to the moment when war was unavoidable. After 1871, knowing that war would spell disaster, he exerted all his ingenuity to seeking diplomatic solutions exclusively. From 1871 to 1890, the more his problems multiplied, the more did his solutions. No man was more infinite in resource, if only because, being quite without principles, no device was barred to him on the grounds of past promises, personal convictions or political commitments. By 1890, indeed, he had toyed with so many devices, that there were very few left for him to think of: worse still, all his devices tended towards the same purpose, that of maintaining himself in power. If he lacked megalomania, he certainly did not lack arrogance. Yet the arrogance was matched by the skill. That, his successors never understood. German policy after him had only the arrogance.

XIII

IMPERIAL CONFLICTS AND EUROPEAN ALIGNMENTS 1875–1907

DURING the Forty Years' Peace after 1815 the Great Powers were afraid of revolution. During the Forty Years' Peace after 1871 they were afraid of one another. It is certainly optimistic to describe Europe in the period after 1890 as in a state of balance between the Triple Alliance and the Franco-Russian Alliance. What Bismarck bequeathed to Europe was not balance but extreme tension, since for one thing the Great Power situation in the west was based on what the French regarded as an act of injustice. Worse still, the injustice that the French saw in the situation was something more than merely the loss of Alsace-Lorraine. The desire for the recovery of the lost provinces, for all their economic and strategic value, was always symbolic of a larger yearning, which peaceful diplomacy could hardly fulfil and only long years of peace suppress, for a restoration to France of her lost status as a first class power. In eastern Europe the situation after 1878 was more dangerous than it had been between 1815 and 1853 because whereas in the earlier period the Ottoman Empire in Europe could still act as a buffer between Germans and Russians, it was rapidly ceasing to serve that purpose and was in process of becoming an obvious *terre à partage*. The growth simultaneously of Pan-Germanism and Pan-Slavism was the necessary consequence of the collapse of the old Holy Alliance. Although Bismarck's Dual Alliance postponed the clash, it could not long disguise the fact that it existed. Worse still, the disputed area was itself now alive with minor nationalisms, which made it very difficult to divide it into spheres of influence like other disputed colonial areas. The bitter rivalries between Greek, Serb and Bulgarian after their release from Turkish control made them dangerously unamenable to control by the Great Powers. On the whole, they inclined towards Russia, whether as the Holy Russia of the Orthodox Faith or as the motherland of the Slavs. Yet tactless handling by Russia, as the example of Bulgaria showed, could cause a Balkan state to display a degree of independence that wrecked even the simplest diplomatic calculations based on the Great Powers' need for peace through partition. Consequently the international situation from 1871 to 1914 was one of intense difficulty. Its two basic problems, Alsace-Lorraine in the west and the Balkans in the east, were of a character that might well make solution by diplomacy impossible.

It is for this reason that the conduct of the Great Powers in dealing with the Balkan problem from 1875 to 1878 appears so clumsy. The Andrassy Note, the Berlin Memorandum, and the Constantinople Conference were attempts to erect mere paper barriers between the Turks and Balkan nationalism, and they all failed. No more than the Greeks in 1821 could the Herzegovinans in 1875 be fobbed off with Turkish promises of reform, unenthusiastically urged by Great Powers whose interest was solely in keeping the Sultan's dominions intact. More significant still, Russia and the Western powers alike were as incapable of controlling Bulgarian nationalism after 1877 as Napoleon III and Cavour had been of controlling Italian nationalism after 1859. The Russians and the West both acted on the assumption that a redeemed Bulgaria would be pro-Russian, only to find by 1885 that it possessed a national will of its own. Hence both Russia and the West found themselves compelled to reverse in 1885 the policies they had respectively pursued in 1878. In 1878 the West nearly fought Russia in order to keep Bulgaria small; in 1886 and 1887 the West nearly fought Russia in order to let Bulgaria be big. The lesson was not that Mr Gladstone had been right in his optimistic belief that the breasts of free men were an adequate barrier against Russia; it was that the breasts of free men contained hearts too passionate to submit to the schemes of Great Power diplomacy even when the aim of that diplomacy was peace. The lesson was underlined when the Serbs in 1885 went to war with Bulgaria solely because the latter had gained Eastern Roumelia. The spectacle amused Mr Bernard Shaw; and out of his amusement came his play *Arms and the Man*. But Balkan nationalism was no joke. It was dynamite; and Bismarck's anxieties over it were a good deal more adult than Bernard Shaw's witticisms. In 1885 Serbia was saved from Bulgaria by an Austrian ultimatum to Sofia; but the Serbo-Bulgarian war was the prologue to a Balkan drama at the end of which an Austrian ultimatum was sent to Belgrade to save Austria from the Serbs.

It is not surprising therefore that from about 1880 until the end of the century, diplomacy, like the churchmen of the Middle Ages diverting the energies of Norman barons to crusading ventures in the east, sought to stimulate the diversion of the aggressive energies of its own age to regions as far from the explosive European scene as possible. In encouraging the French in North Africa, Bismarck showed a profound sense of the urgent need, if peace was to be preserved, of diverting the European (though not the German) mind outwards, away from its own interior conflicts. Similarly, Russia, possessing as she did a vast Asian circumference, turned her eyes increasingly eastward after 1880 and in this she was greatly assisted, after 1890, by French loans. If only Austria-Hungary had had an extra-European sphere of interest war might have been postponed indefinitely. As it was she was worse off even than the Italians, who though without prospects in Europe after their admission into the Triple Alliance, had an answer to their problems of expansion, though a somewhat dusty one, in Tripoli, Eritrea, Somaliland and Abyssinia.

The factors on which the European peace depended after 1878 were therefore both complicated and delicate. To secure the Balkan *status quo*, Austria-Hungary was to be kept dependent upon Berlin by means of the 1879 Dual Alliance. Russia was to be diverted to Asia, and as a further check was to be controlled either by the Three Emperors' League or the devices that succeeded it. It must not be supposed that the ineffectiveness of the Reinsurance Treaty or the rather over-publicized break with Russia when William II dismissed Bismarck ever committed Berlin to a doctrine of unquestioning hostility to Russia. There is hardly a time between 1890 and 1912 when German diplomacy did not keep well in mind the possibility of detaching Russia from France and reviving a Three Emperors' League instead. Indeed it was his lunatic abandonment of this aim of maintaining contact with Russia that constitutes the main burden of the charge against Bülow for sending the virtual ultimatum that humiliated Russia out of the Bosnian affair in 1909; and even thereafter attempts were still being made as late as 1912 to repair the bridge between Berlin and St Petersburg which Bülow had so wantonly mined.

Similarly, Italy was to be kept from threatening the Habsburgs with claims on the Tyrol and the eastern shores of the Adriatic by her imprisonment within the Triple Alliance, but could be vaguely patronized in Africa. France was to be kept as friendless as possible in Europe, but encouraged in Tunis and assisted in the task of embarrassing the British in Egypt. The scheme was rounded off by the assumption that Germany herself would refrain from colonial adventures or from antagonizing England out of her aloofness from Europe.

The implications of this plan for peace therefore were that Germany remained master of Europe on the basis of the *status quo* of 1871 and a dominating army, while the other European powers entangled themselves with one another and with England in the further continents. As for Europe's own colonial problems in the Balkans, they were to be placed in permanent cold storage. It is because most of this complicated machinery for the preservation of European peace was devised by Bismarck and largely survived his fall that he may be regarded rightly as having contributed in great measure to the absence of general war for so long after 1871. It is certainly true that the central fact of international history from 1898 onwards is the collapse of this peace-preserving machinery; and that collapse made European war very difficult and in the end impossible to avoid.

The elementary logic of the extra-European expansion of France and Russia was that it would lead them into difficulties with England. British sensitivity about the Mediterranean and the approaches to India by land and sea were the fundamental principles of world diplomacy as it then existed. On the basis of these principles it was reasonable to calculate that the chief development for the future would be peace in Europe while France and Russia engaged in a complicated struggle with England in Africa and Asia. The only repercussion on European affairs would be a tightening of the existing links between England and the Triple Alliance, on the lines of the Mediterranean Agreement of 1887, agreeing to joint resistance against any Russian encroachments in that area.

The story of international affairs from 1898 to 1907 is the story of how what actually happened turned out to be the opposite of this. England, France and Russia composed their differences outside Europe. By 1907, except for Morocco, no major area of dispute in the colonial sphere outside Europe existed. Yet, so far from making for peace, the elimination of these colonial rivalries by that date had made war much more likely. That part of the apparatus of peace which depended on

France and Russia being engaged in adventures outside Europe had been destroyed.

Yet the crux of the frequently described diplomatic revolution of those years is not England's relations with France and Russia, but her relations with Germany. For although the creation of the Triple Entente certainly meant that England extricated herself from the possibility of war against France and Russia, it need not have implied, as it did, the possibility of England being involved instead in a war against Germany. The really revolutionary circumstance was that the formation of the Triple Entente was accompanied by the transformation of relations between England and Germany; and as a result, not of English, but of German, policy. The diplomatic revolution of the opening years of the nineteenth century was not made in London by Lansdowne, or even in Paris by Delcassé. It was made in Germany.

Unexpected and revolutionary the changes certainly were, though they have perhaps been more frequently described than convincingly explained. The *ententes* with France and Russia, with whom England had then many new and ancient quarrels; her alienation from Germany, with whom she then had no ancient quarrels and no contemporary territorial ones; and, almost by accident, her further alienation from Austria-Hungary with whom she had no quarrel at all—these are properly regarded as startling developments and not as inevitable ones. It was not madness but logic that saw, as an alternative to what happened, an alliance of Teuton and Anglo-Saxon—England, Germany and the United States—against Latin and Slav. For that, as late as 1900, could be considered a reasonable diplomatic deduction from the available data of world facts. That this solution was not achieved, and, as it turned out, could not be secured in the circumstances of the time, is the determining factor in the history of Europe and the world in the first half of the twentieth century. The idea of it, obscured, distorted and partial, may not unreasonably be detected operating—for a second time with a lack of success that determined world history—in the policy that led to the Munich agreement in 1938. And a half-century after its first exposition and abandonment it re-appeared in a new and strange form in 1950; perhaps to provide, whether by its success or failure, a key to the history of the twentieth century's second half.

The starting point of the diplomatic changes of the period was the uneasy feeling in England in the last years of the nineteenth century that something required to be done to strengthen the security of the British Empire. The need was felt, initially, as a matter of naval supremacy. This is not, as it is sometimes represented, merely a matter of England reacting violently to the creation of the German navy. It was rather that in the last quarter of the nineteenth century the economic and strategic resources of the United Kingdom were felt to be in danger of becoming over-strained in consequence of the several major alterations which had taken place in the balance of world forces since about 1860. The conclusion of the American Civil War began the release of the enormous economic potentialities of the United States. The reaction upon British agriculture was immediate and was seen as a clear indication of worse to come in the future; and, diplomatically, Anglo-United States relations were chronically unfriendly. In the vital strategic sphere of the Mediterranean, the situation seemed to some minds to have worsened, though it may well be that these fears were exaggerated. France was astride its western end; Italy had emerged in the centre; and as a potential naval ally against France and Russia was far too weak to be of real value, though strong enough to complicate the situation. It was believed in some quarters that England was incapable of defending the Mediterranean against the French and Russian fleets, and this at a time when the

Mediterranean was more important than ever owing to the lengthening of British communications consequent upon the opening up of the African continent. At the eastern end of the Mediterranean, the Russian threat to Constantinople was still not yet regarded officially as a thing of the past and the British occupation of Egypt was continually harassed by unfriendly French and German diplomacy. In central Asia, Russia still seemed to menace Afghanistan and Persia. In the Far East, the Japanese revolution of 1867 had created one new power in the China Sea, while the construction of Vladivostok, and Russian ambitions in Manchuria, held the threat of the creation of yet another still more dangerous. On the traditional sea route to India and China, British security was menaced by the independence of the Boers, behind whom, and indeed among whom, stood hostile Germans; and only uncertain Siam lay between India and uneasily-held Burma and a French advance westwards from Indo-China. Add to these the growing industrial and naval strength of Germany, and it can be seen that the United Kingdom faced a multitude of problems in the last quarter of the nineteenth century. To the accompaniment of intractable industrial and agricultural problems at home, the world economic, strategic and naval situation had become potentially much more dangerous. The enormous and unprecedented monopoly of power which the United Kingdom had enjoyed between 1815 and 1865, and which the mid-Victorians had thought part of the natural order of things, was everywhere threatened.

There was one school of thought which advocated the acceptance of the changed world situation as a challenge to be overcome. It gave rise to the Imperialist notions embodied most conspicuously in Chamberlain and Rhodes. These were men who reacted to the prospect of a struggle for world power by proposing that it should be fought. They wanted to fight it economically by protection; colonially, by the resolute absorption of as much of Africa as possible, and by a firm determination to maintain India and the China trade at all costs against the Russians; and diplomatically by an association with the United States and Germany, the two powers with whom we had no serious overseas differences and who appeared most capable of realistically agreeing to a partitioning of the world and most capable of defending such a partition against the French and Russians.

To advocate this policy was in fact to propose a realistic British counterpart of the *Weltpolitik* of the Germans. It could not be realized in practice because, in the state of opinion then existing, it was on all counts premature. What was at best an intelligent anticipation of what might conceivably happen given the continuing development of the world tendencies then existing, was not practical politics in the world as it actually was in 1900. Partnership between the United States and the United Kingdom could be tolerated in the United States only when it was much clearer than it was that the British were no longer the world's most powerful Imperialists. Any involvement in Europe was impossible for Americans, since the United States was an organization whose members had entered it because their profoundest wish was to escape from Europe and the burdens which Europe's history had imposed on them—burdens such as unemployment in the United Kingdom, the poverty of Ireland and Italy, and the deadweight of national and racial persecution in eastern Europe. When Henry Ford said 'History is bunk' he showed a profound historical understanding; for the United States had been founded and nurtured on the principle that history as it had hitherto been known and endured in Europe was something to be utterly discarded. Association between the United States and the United Kingdom would have been a betrayal of the Declaration of Independence; association with a European power would have been a betrayal of the Monroe Doctrine, which was America's declaration of independence from Europe. The nation that believed it had fought itself free from history would never capitulate to it until history had plainly ceased to be European history and become world history.

For their part, the Germans had come much sooner than the United States to the conclusion that the British Empire was in decline; but in 1900 they did not think it had yet declined enough, and their cocksure brand of realism told them that sooner or later the British would be compelled to turn to them as suppliants so ready to accept German terms that they could no longer even pretend to be equals in search of a friend.

As for English opinion, it was still lagging well behind events. On one side, the traditional ruling class had no stomach for seeking a fight with anybody, and Lord Salisbury was not undeserving of the epithet 'Byzantine', applied to him by some German diplomats. To hold what was vital, but on the periphery to concede whenever concession appeared politic; to withhold all faith in large remedies; to keep applying the mind to the historic problems such as Turkey, with which he had grown up, and to do as little as possible about new ones, such as China, until there was much more evidence to go on; to make no new friends, since friendship involved obligations and England already had obligations enough; not to treat enmity with Russia and France as a principle to be maintained regardless of the particular issue of the moment—these notions made up Lord Salisbury's policy. Like his nephew, Arthur Balfour, he believed he lived in a singularly ill-contrived world, but that it was not so singularly ill-contrived that broadly conceived dramatic solutions were the only ones.

To the bulk of British opinion, the whole policy of Imperialism was an affront, and the word 'empire' itself was suspect as new-fangled and vulgar, and fit only for Russians and Bulgarians. The existence of colonies constituted an encumbrance which had the unfortunate consequence of causing the Admiralty to make financial demands that embarrassed Chancellors of the Exchequer and perpetuated the Income Tax. The principles of Free Trade made the acquisition of territory unnecessary, and the principles of morality revealed that the possession of Asiatic and African territories constituted an attack on peoples struggling to be free. Against notions such as these, bred into the bones of many mid- and late-Victorian Englishmen, the idea of the special duty of the British to take a pride in bearing the white man's burden or in conferring on Africa and Asia the benefits of Anglo-Saxon civilization by the annexation, exploitation, administration and defence of backward territories and peoples could not make permanent headway, or become the predominant English philosophy. The Imperialists had only to make a few mistakes and they would be permanently discredited among powerful sections of public opinion. And make mistakes they did. The Jameson Raid, the Boer War and Chamberlain's support of Tariff Reform wrecked all chance of the British rallying as a people under the banner of Imperialism. The Boer War in particular confronted the English with the shattering experience of finding themselves universally condemned by a world opinion that based its disapproval on just those principles of liberty which the English were accustomed to invoke against others. The consequence was that, so far from becoming Imperialists, the English entered upon the twentieth century with a sense of shame-faced guilt from which they have never since succeeded in escaping.

The policy actually pursued by the British government from 1898 onwards was not therefore aggressive or ambitious but somewhat anxiously defensive, and not directed towards achieving any major alteration in world affairs. It was intended to be a policy of cautious consolidation and of piecemeal adjustment to the realities of a changing world. The first step was an attempt to deal with the Russian threat to British commercial interests in China and British naval predominance in the China Sea. In 1898 Salisbury proposed a delimitation of British and Russian spheres of influence in Asia, particularly China. The attempt was unsuccessful because the Russians were at that moment bent on the acquisition of Port Arthur and had no intention of being diverted from that aim. Agreement with Russia having proved impossible, and the acquisition of Port Arthur having made the naval situation more serious than ever, Chamberlain made the straightforward deduction that it was necessary to take more vigorous action to check Russia. This would require assistance, and he therefore initiated the first of the various approaches to Germany. It is interesting that when the talks began, Salisbury's health had compelled him to relinquish the Foreign Office for a time. But he naturally knew of the talks, had little hope of their coming to anything, and criticized the proposal for an Anglo-German alliance in much the same terms as French efforts to turn the Entente Cordiale into an alliance were later to be criticized by Grey.

The first difficulty about an agreement between England and Germany was that there was practically nothing that England could offer Germany in return for the latter's assistance against Russia. Bülow is unanswerable on this point. Germany was not at that time threatened by Russia and it would be folly for Germany to put herself in that position of avowed enmity to Russia which an alliance with England would involve, unless there was some strong compensating advantage. If Germany was to guarantee British power in China, it could do so only on the basis that the British would guarantee Germany and Austria-Hungary against Russia. Two objections of Salisbury's make clear that this was felt to be impossible. He declared that the obligation of defending German and Austrian frontiers against Russia was heavier 'than that of defending the British Isles against France'. Second was the objection that England was primarily a naval power; this he had summed up in 1886 in the laconic phrase, 'we are fish'. The British navy could do nothing for Austria-Hungary.

Two other objections existed on the German side and were not unrelated. One was the German belief that war between England and Russia was inevitable. The other was that the Germans were determined not to be deflected from their intention of building a navy. At this stage the purpose of the German naval programme was chiefly to enable Germany to carry more weight as arbiter between England and Russia when the time came for their inevitable conflict. The Germans were not going to be the dupes of British Imperialism. They would let it move towards its destined clash with Russia; and then, at the right diplomatic moment, impose their own terms upon the disputants. Though not a policy of aggression but a typically Prussian one of playing the jackal, it did require, if it was to be effective, the backing of a powerful navy with which to overawe the British, as well as a powerful army with which to overawe the Russians. The role of sea-power in world affairs had after all just been convincingly demonstrated by the United States in their recently concluded war with Spain. Germany would therefore play for time until her navy was ready to enable her to assume the dominating role not only in Europe but also in the world.

There were, all through the period of the attempt from 1898 to 1901 to come to an agreement with Germany, a number of minor irritations which militated against a reasonable settlement. There was the violent hostility of the German press during the Boer War, the American quarrel with the British over Venezuela, a crisis over Samoa, misunderstandings over the Anglo-German treaty of 1900 about China, and British dislike of the Bagdad Railway scheme. None of these problems was comparable in magnitude to those which separated England from France and Russia, and they could have been settled had the Germans not been so sure of themselves or perhaps if the negotiations had not been conducted against the background of the Boer War. This, by revealing Britain's diplomatic isolation and military incompetence, made her appear more of a liability than a potential ally. Yet the governing factor was less these considerations than the German miscalculation that the British had already sunk so low as to have no margin of choice left in their foreign policy. The miscalculation was based on no particularly aggressive intent towards England, but on the mistaken view that the British warning that they would approach France if no satisfaction was to be had from Berlin was merely 'a nightmare invented to frighten' the Germans. Seeing all the world's problems from the point of view of an aggressive and expanding power they failed to comprehend that the aim of the British at that moment was simply to achieve a careful accommodation with difficult realities. If a 'triple alliance' with Germany and the United States was impracticable, they would try something else. The Germans, with no history behind them save forty years of unchallenged success in an undeviating advance to greatness, and looking forward to a future in which they expected as little resistance as they had found in the past, could not help assuming that the decline of England would be as inevitable and as uninterrupted as their own ascent to predominance. They would wait, therefore, for destiny to work itself out. History was on their side, moving towards the moment when England, helpless, would have no alternative but to seek German assistance on Germany's terms. There was nothing in their experience as a nation state to help them to understand the readiness with which the English were prepared to adapt themselves to circumstances. To the Germans, circumstances were a mere anvil and policy a series of irresistible hammer blows shaping the inevitable.

The first consequence of the failure of the German negotiations was the Anglo-Japanese Alliance of 1902. Although widely regarded as marking the end of 'Splendid Isolation' its purpose was rather to avoid ending that isolation. The approach to Germany had confirmed the main thesis of the isolationists, that the price of an alliance with a European power was not a reduction of British commitments, but an increase of them. An alliance with Japan involved no such new commitments in Europe and was sought as a substitute for an agreement with Germany precisely because the latter really would have ended British isolation from Europe. The British aim in the Japanese alliance was the same as that for which agreement with Germany had been sought, the containment of Russia in the Far East; and it had the supreme advantage that its signature left England as free of continental entanglements as ever.

The Japanese alliance had its dangers, certainly; but they were not instantly foreseeable dangers like those involved in association with either the Triple or Dual Alliances. It involved United States disapproval, and it carried the possibility of England being involved in resisting on behalf of Japan a Russian aggression against Korea. It also failed, when first signed, to secure as a *quid pro quo* for this British commitment in Korea any similar Japanese commitment to support England in the event of a two-power threat to India. It is an indication that Lansdowne clearly felt that the British could not afford to be too nice in their calculations. The problem of naval power in the Far East had to be tackled, and as the only available means of dealing with it, the Japanese alliance had to be accepted despite its drawbacks.

As it turned out, few diplomatic moves have achieved the desired end so quickly, for with the treaty in their pockets the Japanese were ready for war with the Russians and within three years of the treaty's signature the British aim of the destruction of Russian sea power in the Far East had been attained. One of England's major imperial problems had been swiftly and decisively solved. Yet the solution would make the preservation of the general peace not easier but harder. There were limits to the extent to which Russia could be contained in this way. For, though Russia could perhaps put up with being thwarted in Afghanistan or in the Far East, this made it all the harder for her to accept rebuffs in the Balkan area. This tendency to constrict to the Balkans the area in which Russia could conduct an effective foreign policy in public would shortly be intensified by the agreement with England over Persia in 1907. After that there could be no more crises in Asia, but only in the Balkans; and it was precisely over Balkan problems that the Russian government, for fear of public opinion, could least afford to compromise. Superficially, there is a case for saying that the Anglo-Japanese Alliance and the Russo-Japanese war, by preventing the Russians from attempting to expand in the Far East beyond Manchuria, merely stopped them from doing something they were not capable of doing. But by inflicting on the Russian government a spectacular humiliation, the Anglo-Japanese move helped to create in Russia the restlessness that provoked Izvolsky into the course of conduct that produced the Bosnian crisis. That was a humiliation for Russia, too: but it turned out to be the last that the Russians put up with. In short, the Far Eastern crisis, followed as it was by the Persian agreement with England, which compelled Russia to advance in Persia exclusively in secret, made it more difficult for Russia to turn her back on Europe, even though there were many Russians who wanted her to do so.

The likelihood of an enforced Russian concentration on the Balkans would have been less dangerous if it had not been accompanied by the achievement of a British triumph over the French similar to the triumph over the Russians. For Fashoda did to the French what the Russo-Japanese war did to the Russians. It brought them face to face (and not by proxy, as happened to the Russians) with the realization of what a policy of imperial expansion involved if it was pursued to the point where the British were determined to resist. When Marchand hauled down the French flag at Fashoda, the French found themselves turned back towards Europe in the same degree as Russia was turned back in the same direction by the Treaty of Portsmouth. Earlier, a French imperialist had declared, 'Colonization is for France a question of life and death: either France becomes a great African power, or in a century or two she will be no more than a secondary European power; she will count for about as much in the world as Greece or Roumania in Europe.' It was a fair enough statement of the probabilities. But Fashoda made public the fact that the price of further African expansion was a war with England. The price was one the French could not pay. It was extremely unlikely that they would get Russian support for a war against England over Egypt and the Sudan, and very uncertain what that support would be worth if they ever got it. In fact, Fashoda called the French bluff in the Sudan as dramatically as Palmerston had called their bluff over Syria in 1840.

It was at this point that Delcassé entered the story. Even though she found herself thwarted in Africa, France had still no mind to be a mere Greece or Roumania, and it was Delcassé's aim to reassert French prestige in Europe, to escape, that is, from that position of subordination to Germany the logical outcome of which, as Fashoda had demonstrated, was a war against England which France had no hope of fighting. The only feasible policy for the French after Fashoda was to drop their bluff and come to an agreement with England.

Lansdowne accepted the notion of an *entente* with France as eagerly as that of an alliance with Japan. French hostility to the British occupation of Egypt had been deliberately used by the Germans as a means of embarrassing the British; the German attitude had been, according to Grey, that the English were on such bad terms with France over Egypt that they could not afford to be difficult with the Germans. Faced therefore with the immediate prospect of settling North African difficulties as neatly as those of the Far East had been settled, Lansdowne accepted the *entente* with alacrity, particularly as it also provided a useful insurance against the French joining the Russians in the war with Japan. This particular point weighed a great deal with Delcassé. The existence of the Anglo-Japanese alliance made it possible that France would find herself at war with England after all—as Russia's ally against Japan's ally. This, Delcassé was determined to avoid. Quite apart from being the logical outcome of Fashoda, the *entente* was, to Delcassé, an attempt to prevent an open breach between Russia and England which might lead to the French having to fight Russia's battles. He also saw it, and this is most significant, as a prelude to a triple association of the three Powers which would balance the Triple Alliance from which, as far as France was concerned, he had already succeeded in detaching Italy in 1902. He was not, of course, aiming at a war with anybody; quite the reverse. Like the British at this time, he was merely pursuing the well worn paths of diplomatic routine.

From the British point of view the *entente* cleared the whole field of Anglo-French colonial problems as successfully as the Japanese alliance had swept the Russians out of the China Sea.

England had solved the main problems of imperial consolidation and security, and had done so without German assistance and without membership of either of the European alliances. Lansdowne had every reason to congratulate himself on a diplomatic achievement that would have hardly seemed possible during the time of the Boer War, for instance.

Yet the triumphs of British policy in the colonial field between 1902 and 1904 were less revolutionary than they looked because the dangers they averted were less spectacular than they looked. The Anglo-Japanese alliance had led to the revelation that the Russian navy was not even a match for the Japanese navy, let alone the British. In abandoning their claims on Egypt in 1904 the French were, after all, only giving up something they were never likely to get. Nor was the notion of diplomatic co-operation with France the unprecedented novelty it appeared to those whose minds, jumping back from Fashoda across the intervening centuries to Agincourt, Blenheim and Trafalgar, overlooked the more recent collaboration between the two countries under Palmerston and Aberdeen. Of itself, the *entente* was not a revolution in Anglo-French relations, though given that the public's memory in England went no further back than Fashoda, and in France no further back than the Boer War, it seemed to be one; and this is a reminder that if Edward VII was not the architect of the *entente* in the diplomatic sense, he was in the sphere of public relations.

This difference between the public view of the *entente* and the official view of it, like the difference between its purposes and its consequences, is a reminder that it is possible to be a little too haughty about public opinion when analysing the diplomatic manœuvres of this period. Now that mass illiteracy was decreasing and the journalist was emerging as a creator and echo of public opinion on a much larger scale than before, the superficial in foreign affairs often came to acquire a greater importance than the underlying reality as seen in the minds of foreign ministers and diplomats. This fact is painful both to politicians and to the historians who write about them; for the journalist infuriates both politicians and historians by enjoying a much wider audience than they do, yet without having to do a tithe of their spinning of memoranda and monographs or of their toiling among the archives and blue books. But professional jealousy of journalists and an academic distaste for the tendency of the public mind to jump to the wrong conclusion on the basis of an imperfect comprehension of the facts must not cause either the power of journalists or the misty minds of the masses to be ignored in the writing of history.

The 'facts' are that the *entente* did not revolutionize Anglo-French or Anglo-German relations. But this conclusion, appropriate enough to a study of what foreign office officials thought and intended, is inadequate. It is like saying that there was nothing revolutionary in the summoning of the States-General in France in 1789; it is only true as far as it goes. Lansdowne, and then Grey, failed to realize what Bülow had realized when Chamberlain had suggested an Anglo-German agreement. Bülow had refused to be put in a position of public hostility towards Russia which at the moment was England's enemy rather than Germany's. Lansdowne does not seem to have realized in 1904 that partnership with France at once put England into just such a position of public hostility towards Germany; and at this stage Germany was the opponent of France and not of England. France, despite the limitations which the *entente* had placed on her colonial policy, was in no mind to become a Greece or Roumania, and it was short-sighted to suppose, as the British appear to have supposed, that Morocco was so insulated from the rest of the world that France could be supported diplomatically there without this involving at least great friction with Germany. Moreover, the *entente*'s exclusion of France from Egypt made French ambitions in Morocco more urgent than ever; for the price of abandoning them would be the final sacrifice of her African ambitions, which she could not tolerate.

All the same, it takes two to make a quarrel; and the real diplomatic revolution came after the *entente*. It came with the decision of the Germans to launch the Tangier crisis in 1905. Of all the well-known events from 1898 onwards, this is the only one that clearly involved anything new and decisive. The passing of the German Navy Law in 1898 did not endanger British naval supremacy; the failure of the Anglo-German negotiations between 1898 and 1901 proved only a negative; Fashoda proved the obvious, and the Anglo-French *entente* wrote it into a treaty; the Anglo-Japanese Alliance was aimed at maintaining England's isolation and not at ending it; the Russo-Japanese war, like Russia's nineteenth century wars against Turkey, prevented the Russians biting off more than they could chew. But the Tangier crisis turned the Anglo-French *entente* into a virtual alliance against Germany. Between 1898 and 1904, the European scene changed hardly at all. A conflict between Triple Alliance and Dual Alliance was no more, and no less, probable in 1904 than in 1898. In 1904 English participation in a continental war on continental soil was as remote a possibility as in 1898. Yet, as a result of the Tangier crisis, such a possibility was envisaged in the Anglo-French staff conversations of 1906; the despatch of the Kaiser to Tangier had the effect of transforming the *entente* from an engagement that only appeared to be anti-German into one that might easily become anti-German in reality.

Thus the dismissal of Delcassé was an empty triumph for the Germans. The policy of trying to break the *entente* by exposing to the English the weakness of the French under pressure did not in fact succeed. It suddenly presented the

English with the prospect of having to face German hostility in isolation, and they reacted accordingly; not by abandoning the French but by upholding them. Accordingly, a mere eleven months after the *entente* had been signed, Lansdowne and Cambon were already having the first of those numerous Anglo-French conversations which took place at intervals until 1914, in which the French sought to persuade the English into admitting an obligation to defend France against Germany while the English replied 'no' in terms that, as time went on, came more and more to mean very little less than 'yes'. As it was, all Europe rang in 1905 with the rumour that the British response to William II's visit to Tangier had been the offer to the French of an offensive and defensive alliance.

From a practical point of view, very little tangible was at stake for Germany in Morocco, and no consideration other than prestige entered into their calculations. The Kaiser's inability to understand just why he was ever sent to Morocco does him credit; but for Bülow, the mere question of prestige was enough in itself. In words that oddly rehearse those of Lloyd George's Mansion House speech during the second Moroccan crisis, Bülow said, 'Our aim was to show that Germany was not to be treated as a negligible quantity.' Not that this testy nervousness about their prestige in colonial affairs was in itself a new departure for the Germans. It had been in evidence many times already, and their attitude to the British in such matters had been an unpleasant mixture of snivelling and blustering, whose burden was chiefly, 'It's not fair that you should have all those colonies while we have hardly any, and unless you arrange for us to add to our overseas empire we shall make ourselves thoroughly awkward.' This had been the German line only recently over the reversion of the Portuguese colonies and about Samoa; a naïve yet sinister disposition to claim that the British had some responsibility for the German failure to achieve national unity until after the creation of the British Empire. But whereas these challenges had been offered to an isolated England, the challenge in 1905 was made to an England which, in the area under dispute, was in association with France. This would necessarily have the effect of making the Anglo-French association stronger instead of weaker, and stronger than either the English or the French had perhaps ever intended it to be.

Equally novel was the break with the tradition that Germany did not seek quarrels with France in the colonial sphere at all; and the necessary consequence of Germany's spectacular interference in Morocco was to make it seem that Germany was pursuing the French with a malice that now knew no frontiers. The French had lost Alsace-Lorraine and the leadership of Europe to the Germans, and saw little chance of ever getting back either. They had formally abandoned Egypt to the British because there was no chance of ever getting Egypt back. Now they were not even going to be allowed the consolation prize of Morocco.

It is a measure of the sudden and revolutionary character of the German intervention that it threw both the French and the British into such extraordinary disarray. The French were caught in two minds: between a policy of resistance to Germany because of this alarming extension of German ambition, and one of agreement with her. They could not resist because they lacked the power, and so Delcassé had to resign. But they could not give way, because if the new German departure meant what it seemed to mean, they would be grateful even of English support, and they could not get that by leaving England to face Germany alone. For their part the English wavered between denying that they had anything more than the merest Moroccan obligation to France and attempting to explore the problem of how to meet a wider and military obligation against Germany if there proved no escape from it.

And the English, too, found themselves pushing the French on at one stage, for fear of having to face Germany in isolation. Anglo-French policy in the first Moroccan crisis was thoroughly incoherent because both the English and the French were faced with a situation for which they were entirely unprepared.

For their part, the Germans had only themselves to blame if their action gave rise to fears about them which at the time could be represented as exaggerated. But in customary human manner, while they threatened the French, they tended to make the British the real culprits. The British thought the behaviour of the Germans surprising and unjustifiable; the Germans thought the same about British behaviour. It was monstrous that the British with their huge empire should associate with France in denying Germany her rightful share of Moroccan influence: and the feeling towards the British in some quarters in Germany was described as one of 'rancorous hatred'. For the end of it was that Bülow's move to assert German prestige failed. The Germans did not get their own way at Algeciras; because of the British, the Reich had known diplomatic defeat for the first time in its history; and *The Times* published a leading article headed 'The Isolation of Germany'.

Yet again British diplomacy had won a bigger victory than ever it had intended. The Anglo-Japanese alliance, limited in aim, had destroyed the Russian Far Eastern fleet. Now, the Anglo-French *entente*, even more limited in aim, had put the British in the position of diplomatic victors over the Germans, hitherto always accustomed to being victors themselves. It is hard to avoid comparing the British to careless picnickers who, thinking to light a little fire on which to cook themselves a modest meal, find they have started a whole forest fire.

The logic of a policy that had now committed them to the possibility (however remote) of a military clash with Germany was a reversal of policy towards Russia. The shock to the chaotic Romanov state administered by the victories of the Japanese and by the 1905 Revolution meant that Russia must for the time being cease to be a threat to peace in Asia. An agreement with Russia at this particular juncture therefore could possess real relevance only in Europe. Its purpose could only be that of preventing her either from siding with Germany or from ceasing, through financial and social collapse, from being an adequate partner for the French in a struggle against Germany. There was a good deal of truth in H. N. Brailsford's comment at the time, 'Had peace been our object we should have sought it rather in Berlin than in St Petersburg'. The Russian *entente* was not planned with peace in view at all: it was planned solely with reference to the possibility of trouble with Germany. Grey was never at much pains to defend the specifically Persian terms of the Russian *entente*. He admitted that it did not limit in the slightest Russia's control of northern Persia; and, later, that Russia failed to respect the agreement in regard to the 'neutral' sphere of Persia. He took it for granted that however unsatisfactory it was in itself the agreement about Persia was the necessary price to be paid for keeping Russia on the side of the French and the English in Europe.

The signature of the Anglo-Russian *entente* is a measure of the distance that had been travelled since the Germans had refused an agreement with England less than ten years before, in the confident expectation that the English must sooner or later find themselves at war with Russia. Indeed, the whole story of the revolution in international relations between 1898 and 1907 is a most valuable object lesson on the unwisdom of pompous theories about the 'inexorable' march of events or about 'inevitable' tendencies.

It is appropriate at this point to consider the relevance of the development of the German navy to England's diplomatic revolution. The needs of naval defence do not provide quite as clear-cut an explanation of the change as one might expect. Until 1902 the naval problem was still seen as a matter of Mediterranean defence against the combined fleets of France and Russia, and of defence against Russia in the China Sea; just as for some time afterwards the purpose of any expeditionary force was thought to lie in the defence of the North-West Frontier of India, and not of France and Belgium. The Japanese alliance and the Anglo-French *entente* seem to have been concluded with these naval problems in mind, rather than the German navy specifically, although the latter had an important secondary relevance. The alliance and the *entente* permitted the withdrawal of ships from the China Sea and the Mediterranean, and also permitted the beginning in 1905 of the process of concentrating British naval forces within the Atlantic, Channel and Home Fleets as a counter to Germany. But this altered fleet disposition, together with the laying down of the first Dreadnought in 1905, gave the British an enormous naval lead over the Germans; and if the Dreadnought programme had been carried out by the Liberals on the scale originally planned by the Conservatives in 1905 it would have given the British a naval lead which it is considered the Germans could not have hoped to overtake. As it was, the building of the Dreadnoughts postponed the possibility of effective naval action by Germany in the North Sea until the opening of the Kiel Canal in 1914. It appears that at any rate until 1908 the German naval programme, though a threat, was not a mortal one, and it either did not dictate, or ought not to have dictated, British foreign policy, until well after the material decisions had been taken and their consequences revealed by the Tangier crisis.

In summary, it may be said that the British adjusted themselves in the only way that seemed possible to the Russian threat in China, to French hostility in Africa and to the German threat in the North Sea. They thought strictly in terms of naval and imperial defence and hardly at all of Europe. Faced at the Tangier crisis with the hostility of the Germans, they suddenly saw, and accepted, the implications of what they had done. If the agreement with France failed, there would be no agreement with Russia: and as things then stood a renewal of Russian friendship with Germany was the probable outcome. France might then feel compelled to associate with those powers in an anti-British coalition of the sort that had been meditated during the Boer War and which reappeared as a possibility to both William II and Bülow during the Anglo-Japanese war and also to the Russian minister Witte at the same time. The British had no alternative but to base all their policy henceforth on a determination to maintain France as a Great Power in Europe, even if the cost of so doing involved the maintenance of Russia also, and in due course the possibility of a head-on collision with Germany.

XIV

CRY HAVOC . . . 1907–1914

FEW foreign secretaries have faced more difficulties than those which faced Sir Edward Grey from 1906 to 1914 and few grappled with them more steadfastly. The first of the various charges from which Grey should be exonerated is that of insufficient concentration, a charge based on the somewhat irritating frequency with which he expressed his preference for bird-watching at Fallodon compared with his duties at the Foreign Office. The evidence is rather that this was no more than an oblique and wholly creditable method of expressing his sense of the magnitude of his task and of the distastefulness of the men and the tendencies he had to deal with as Foreign Secretary. To express, however frequently, a preference for studying the habits of wild birds and ornamental ducks in the midst of a working life devoted to coping with the consequences of policies controlled (if that is the right word) by men as unreliable as William II, Bülow, Kiderlen-Wächter, Aehrenthal, Conrad von Hoetzendorf, Izvolsky and the rest is evidence not of idleness but of an acute and understandable sense of strain.

The second charge of which he should be acquitted is that he failed to make it plain to the Germans that England would intervene with a continental army if Germany attacked France. That this would in fact happen had been the confident expectation of every diplomat and observer since the Tangier incident, and the Germans had been told plainly and in terms that it would happen. The Schlieffen plan assumed the participation of a British force. The German calculation in 1914 was not that England would be neutral but that English military intervention would not matter. What the Germans did not know in 1914 was that the participation of England would contribute materially to the defeat of their plan to beat the French in six weeks, and would lead to the eventual mobilization of the whole British Empire and the United States against Germany. In short, the only thing the Germans did not know in 1914 was that they were going to lose the war. The attempt, after the event, to put the blame for their own miscalculation on Grey was one of the more transparent of German propaganda devices.

The associated criticism that Grey should have turned the *entente* into a formal alliance is equally misguided. The only purpose of so doing would be to leave the Germans in no doubt of British intentions; but they were in no doubt anyway and did not really care. Grey's insistence on an *entente* rather than an alliance preserved for British foreign policy its only remaining margin of choice, its sole chance of fending off what appeared otherwise inevitable. Of course the French were importunate, for their existence was at stake; but an alliance with France would have meant an alliance with Russia, and to allow British action to become dependent upon the men around the Romanovs would have been criminally stupid.

A third criticism is that he failed to take public opinion into his confidence, particularly in the matter of the staff conversations of 1906 and the fleet dispositions of 1912. The argument runs that he was binding this country to France without frankly telling the public what he was doing. Yet this overlooks almost the greatest of Grey's difficulties, the fact that he was Foreign Secretary of a Liberal Government, which had a strong Radical element and which was dependent for its long-term political future on its ability to be, or to appear to be, as 'progressive' and 'enlightened' as the Labour party and its

Socialist and proletarian supporters. The consequence was that Grey conducted his foreign policy in the full knowledge that many people within his own party, some inside the Cabinet, and the bulk of his party's political allies in England did not believe that the international problems he had to deal with had any real existence. So far was it from practical politics to have a formal alliance with France and Russia that Grey could not be sure of adequate parliamentary and newspaper support for the *ententes* with France and Russia even from his own side.

It is true that the decision to create a Triple Entente was open to the objection that it involved England in open opposition to Germany with whom, at the outset, our quarrels were relatively few and to Austria-Hungary with whom we had no quarrel at all. But the decision to make the *entente* into a virtual anti-German alliance was made in Berlin and not in London, by Bülow and not by Lansdowne and Grey. This cardinal fact was always overlooked by Grey's left wing critics. From the moment the Kaiser landed at Tangier the only alternative to maintaining the *entente* was the possibility of a world war in which England was without allies. That may well have been the truth from the moment Germany rejected the overtures of Chamberlain. Agreement with Germany had then been revealed as possible only by agreeing to permanent German blackmail: and given the power-drunk attitude of the Germans, any agreement with France and Russia would almost certainly alienate the Germans, since they had already chosen of their own free will to pursue a policy of cowing the French and were about to choose, equally of their own free will, to cow the Russians.

Grey's progressive, neutralist and pacifist opponents failed to see that their various objections to the *entente* were valid only on the assumption that Germany was sanely governed and possessed a normal degree of good will and moderation.

But this was not so; and the whole progressive case against Grey breaks down since it did in fact assume that Germany was a more civilized state than Russia and a less imperialist one than France. Indeed, half a century's reflection failed to convince a leading contemporary opponent of Grey, H. N. Brailsford, otherwise. In a newspaper article in 1954 on the fiftieth anniversary of the Anglo-French *entente* he declared that it represented British imperialism and French imperialism 'joining forces at their zenith'. It would be difficult to misread the facts more completely. The *entente* was, if not signed, at any rate maintained, because France felt that she had no future without it, and the British that the days when they could maintain their imperial security in isolation were over.

To reveal the full facts to a parliament confused by misconceptions of this sort would have wrecked all of what hope remained of avoiding war or avoiding defeat when it came. Had Grey been as frank as his critics demanded he might have been turned out of office; and the heightened political tension that would have followed would have prevented England from exercising any influence on foreign affairs at all. The public mind was furiously concentrated on social and parliamentary reform, on industrial strikes, on votes for women and home rule for Ireland. If to these had been added an irresponsible and ultimately pointless political controversy about the wickedness of British and French capitalists and imperialists, about the evils of Czarist tyranny and the immorality of dividing Africa and Asia into spheres of influence, and about the monstrous iniquity of building battleships, it is difficult to see how this would have led to anything but social anarchy and perhaps revolution in internal affairs, with a super-Munich in foreign affairs. Whatever else it would have led to, it would have done nothing to improve the social welfare of the Moroccans, the Egyptians, the Persians or the Russians, for whose poverty and misery the progressive forces in England were so keenly concerned.

As it was, risks grave enough were run, and mistakes enough were made, by the influence that these notions had both on Grey and on the Liberal Government. Cuts in naval construction were made, partly to appease the advocates of social reform, and partly out of deference to the quaint theory that the best way to stop the Germans building ships was to show them that England meant them no harm. A similar belief that he might be able to win the Germans over by kindness prompted Grey to take the side of the Germans and Austro-Hungarians at the London Conference that endeavoured to control the effects of the Balkan Wars. As early as 1900 Bülow himself had noticed how ignorant the English were of the reality of Germany's dislike of them; and as late as 1914 the English were persuaded by the amiable attitudes of the German Ambassador, Lichnowsky, and of Bethman-Hollweg into supposing that, compared with the unreliable French and the savage Russians, the German government was composed of gentlemen.

The division of Europe into two armed camps after 1907 meant that henceforward no major international problem could be dealt with on its merits. Instead, each had to be dealt with primarily as a test: a test of each power's loyalty to its allies, of each side's strength to defeat the aims of the other side. So far from international relations being in a state of anarchy it became in the end possible to predict with mathematical accuracy that the behaviour of all of them would be governed rigidly by the pre-determining existence of the two major power-groups. A close-knit and genuinely international organization might preserve the general peace, though the proposition is purely hypothetical; a condition of complete international anarchy is also likely to preserve the general peace, and the Crimean War and the absence of general war between 1859 and 1871 appear to support this view; but a system of alliances such as prevailed just before 1914 seems almost to guarantee a succession of crises likely to produce war.

Given the fairly rigid character of the two groups when facing each other, the only hope for peace was a determination on both sides to raise no major issue which endangered the interests of any power on the other side. The only other method would have been somehow to build a bridge across the great divide, by means of which normal relations could be carried on, or on which the contestants could from time to time meet as it were as neutrals.

For not only did the two camps fail to operate with absolute solidarity even at moments of crisis; between the crises, tension eased very considerably. Indeed, Bülow described Franco-German relations between Algeciras and Agadir as 'sunny'. This was rather optimistic of him; but to describe Anglo-French relations in the same years as sunny would have been hardly less optimistic. Similarly, Austro-Russian relations were relatively amiable before the Bosnian crisis and not irrevocably hostile after it. As for the Triple Alliance itself, it was always liable to be endangered by the importunities of the Habsburg general staff, who up to 1908 had never relinquished the hope of restoring Austrian greatness by a war to win back Lombardy from their Italian ally. Moreover, according to all sane calculations the Triple Alliance might also be gravely threatened if the Habsburg army took the bit between its teeth and embarked on adventures in the Balkans, for such a policy made nonsense of Berlin's alliance with Vienna. As for Russia and Germany, the breach between them had always, at government level, been somewhat artificial, and was intended to imply no more than a warning from the German side against any Russian venturings to the detriment of the Austrians. The English for their part were for some time suspicious of a Franco-German deal in Morocco, sympathetic to the Dual Monarchy, hostile to the Serbs on account of the murder of the Obrenovich King and Queen in 1903, and highly critical of Russia's machinations in Persia. They were also admirers of the Germans as a sober, pious, hard-working people, and were desperately anxious to prove to them that they had no desire for war.

Any postponement of conflict might also have given time for the situation to be affected more decisively by the internal politics of the various powers. With the possible exception of Germany all the powers were in a chaotic state internally. England and France were a prey to industrial disorder, and England had the prospect of civil war in Ireland. Russia was stumbling through a twilight of social and moral collapse, the Dual Monarchy rent by the strife of German against Magyar and of each against Slavs and Roumanians. Thus, those who supposedly ruled the Romanov and Habsburg empires might be expected to realize that for them war was at best a counsel of desperation, with utter destruction as its probable outcome; but any step that tightened the alliance system had the dangerous effect of making each of them think rather of the automatic obligation of their allies to help them than of the internal conditions that made war no more than a gamble. For their part, the governments of England and France faced a degree of proletarian hostility to any warlike move quite without parallel in the period before 1939 when it was the ruled rather than their rulers who most firmly supported resistance to Germany.

Thus, as war machines, both Triple Alliance and Triple Entente were a good deal more ramshackle than they seem in retrospect and, given long enough, both might have disintegrated, either through the centrifugal forces which operate against all alliances, or through the paralysis of more than one of them by internal dissension. Therefore the significance of the crises is that each served to give both of the opposing systems a new lease of life as a tightly drawn combination which dare not act as anything other than an automatic alliance for the unhesitating support, to the point of war, of the prestige of any of its members. It is also reasonable, since the crises were deliberately engineered, to classify those who engineered them as among history's more dangerous criminals.

Peace was always a possibility provided Russia and Austria-Hungary could be kept in a state of balance in the Balkans. This was so elementary that even the governments of the two states were able to realize it; and they had pledged themselves in 1897 and by the Mürzsteg agreement of 1903 to preserve the Balkan *status quo*. In this necessary piece of statecraft Germany had concurred, in loyalty to the Bismarckian precept that Austria-Hungary must serve as a buffer against Russia in the Balkans, not as a battering ram. Given the tense state of European relations after 1907, and given also that Bülow, Aehrenthal and Izvolsky all professed to believe ardently in maintaining the Balkan peace it is difficult to avoid condemning as criminal the way in which they did their best to wreck it for good over the Bosnian affair in 1908.

Given patience and a statesmanlike realization that both matters could most satisfactorily be attained by a revival of the concert of Europe, the aims of Austria-Hungary in Bosnia-Herzegovina and of Russia in the Straits could have been realized without substantial difficulty. The Austrians could have relied on Grey's ignorance of Balkan matters and on England's lack of sympathy with the Serbs; the Russians could have relied in the end on Grey's gentlemanly anxiety to prove that he was truly Russia's friend. Instead, both Izvolsky and Aehrenthal, for reasons exclusively of personal and political prestige, decided on a course of action whose inevitable consequence would be to enrage friends and allies alike.

Aehrenthal's conduct was the more reprehensible, since it does appear that Izvolsky intended to have the matter regulated by conference. Aehrenthal, however, was bent on restoring what he called the independence of the Dual Monarchy by acting alone. This is shown by his readiness to break the Austro-Russian Balkan *entente* by securing the Sanjak railway concession just before the Bosnian crisis developed: this amounted to risking good relations with Russia for the sake of a railway that could not be built anyway. It is shown also by his insistence that the ultimate purpose of annexing Bosnia-Herzegovina was to pave the way for the destruction of the Serb kingdom altogether. Thwarted in Bosnia-Herzegovina, Serbia would turn increasingly towards Macedonia. This would lead to another war between Serbia and Bulgaria; and this time Vienna would act in Belgrade, not to save Serbia, but to help destroy it. To embark on even the first stage of such a reckless programme in such a manner that Russia would not be able to secure even the discussion of her *quid pro quo* of the opening of the Straits was an indication that Aehrenthal had learned nothing from the recent past of the Habsburg empire and understood nothing of the realities of the European situation around him.

That Austria-Hungary should seek to pursue an independent policy of Balkan adventure calculated to involve a clash with Russia was the negation of the purpose of the Austro-German alliance of 1879. That the annexation of Bosnia-Herzegovina should have been planned without previous notice to Berlin was as flagrant a breach of the rules of behaviour between allies as could be imagined. Yet, despite his initial annoyance, Bülow suddenly decided to end the agitated protests of the Russians by sending St Petersburg what amounted to an ultimatum. The move was devoid of statesmanship and can only be explained as Bülow's last attempt to revive his fallen reputation by relying on the only device known to the German political tradition, that of a blatant display of sheer power, allied to no principle whatever. Bülow's senseless support of Aehrenthal over Bosnia was a public announcement that Germany's avowed policy of fearing God and nothing else was in reality one of trying to make all Europe fear Germany and nothing else. The Bosnian annexation and Germany's support of it should have convinced even the most vigorous opponents of the *entente* in England that the real threat to the freedom of backward peoples came from Berlin and Vienna. The imperialist threat to Asians and Africans was as nothing compared with the imperialist threat to the Slavs.

Having, without valid reason, administered a public humiliation to the Russians, the Germans turned, in 1911, to challenging the English to a public trial of strength over Morocco. Not that they intended to do this. They were intelligent enough to be alarmed at the sensation their action had caused in 1909, and what they thought they were doing was combining an attempt at a *détente* with Russia with one more effort to divide England from France. The despatch of the *Panther* to Agadir perfectly reveals the character of German policy: an obtuse belief that it did not matter how brusque, or indeed how ultimately pointless, their behaviour was, because they were so powerful that nobody dare resist them. It was Bülow's ultimatum of 1909 all over again: and the outcome was the same sense of aggrieved shock that it should be taken as an act of aggression. It was silly of the English to imagine that the Germans wanted a naval base at Agadir. Of course they did not. Indeed, Germany did not very seriously want anything tangible at all at this time. They did not even really want trading rights in Morocco, or compensation from the French in central Africa. They merely wanted everybody to go on being frightened of them. They were genuinely upset that Grey should so misunderstand the purpose of the *Panther's* mission as to suppose it had relevance to naval matters when all it was there for was to frighten everyone. They were even more upset to hear Lloyd George speaking in 1911 in the language Bülow had used during the first Moroccan crisis of 1905. It had been right and proper of Bülow to say then that Germany would not allow herself to be treated as 'a negligible quantity'. But it was a breach of everything that Germany stood for for Lloyd George to assert that England would not allow herself to be treated 'as if she were of no account'. For the whole of Bismarckian and post-Bismarckian foreign policy in Germany had been conducted on the basis that in any matter in which Germany concerned herself that was precisely how all other countries should be treated.

It has been objected that it was impolitic for Lloyd George to be allowed to drag the Agadir incident out of the discreet shadows of diplomacy into the glaring light of public controversy. Yet to say this is probably to do no more than to subscribe to the English error of attempting to cure the Germans by kindness, and to ignore what by 1911 had become the central feature of Europe's plight, namely that no matter what messages, whether of concession or defiance, were addressed to Berlin after the fall of Bülow, there was nobody with authority to act upon them. Over the Agadir affair as over Tangier and Bosnia there was no agreed coherent policy in Berlin; and in a very real sense the most important cause of the war of 1914 was not the succession of crises, not the Balkan wars, nor even the Austrian ultimatum to Belgrade, but the complete, though unobserved, collapse of the German system of government.

Bismarck's Reich, as has been seen, was of a character similar to that of Napoleon III's Empire. It depended for its efficient operation on the personal domination either of the German Chancellor or the German Emperor. There was no effective co-ordinating machinery between the various civilian departments and the army and the navy, and no real responsibility to the Reichstag; the system depended for its coherent direction upon the personality, while Bismarck held office, of the Chancellor. When William II dropped Bismarck his intention was to exercise this power of direction and co-ordination himself. This was quite possible and perfectly constitutional, since Bismarck had always claimed to be the servant of the Emperor. In practice, under Bismarck's successors, there was a sort of indeterminate condominium between Emperor and Chancellor, with William striking the attitudes and the Chancellors endeavouring to combine the tasks of managing the Emperor and of manipulating the political blocs in the Reichstag. But in 1908 William was compelled to abdicate his claim to be the All-Highest in fact, and henceforth was so only as a fiction. The occasion of his relegation was the blunder of his celebrated *Daily Telegraph* interview; though the real causes were not unconnected with the jealousy felt by the army leaders at the Emperor's hysterical passion for building a navy. Thereafter a coherent German policy was possible only if the Chancellor was a dominating personality with a clear head and precise aims; or if the Chancellor had become a Prime Minister of a cabinet constitutionally dependent on the Reichstag. But in 1909, Bülow having failed to maintain a majority in the Reichstag, William used the event as an opportunity to dismiss him (though this lack of a majority did not require the Chancellor's resignation). By universal consent Bethman-Hollweg who was appointed to succeed Bülow had no personal qualifications for controlling policy at all. Like Lichnowsky in London, and the many Germans who in 1913 protested against the savagery of the army's treatment of the civilian population in Saverne, in Alsace, Bethman-Hollweg belonged to the category known as 'good' Germans. These were men, however, who did not possess and did not know how to acquire power, to use Shelley's words about good people in general, to do more than 'weep barren tears'.

Amid the collapse of authority caused by this combination of an Emperor without power, a Chancellor without power and a Parliament without power, the army became the only coherent force in Germany. What had never been true under Bismarck had come true now. There was now no authority in Germany but that of the men of blood and iron, and they alone would make the great decisions of the day because nobody else was capable of making decisions. The Bismarckian system had been stood on its head. Under him the army waited upon a diplomacy that in turn served a clearly conceived policy. Now there was neither diplomacy nor policy. Consequently the issue of peace or war would be decided by the army; and on the only basis on which an army could be expected to make decisions—that of simple military calculation as to what was the most militarily favourable moment to fight. And it would not be a war for any purpose beyond that of achieving victory, for what is to be done with victory when it is won is not a soldier's business. Thus Germany had no war aim except victory.

The German authorities also differed from those of the other great powers in having fewer problems of internal morale to hamper them. It was only in Germany that there was any general feeling in favour of a policy of aggression before the war started. It is true that there were anti-militarist groups in Germany, but to transform their pressure into effective restraint upon the government was impossible, since there was almost literally no government to restrain and only a shadow of a parliament by which to restrain it. Hence the only action by which the 'good' Germans could stop war was by direct action—a general strike or a revolution. And what could not happen at the outset of war even in demoralized

Russia or the racially divided Dual Monarchy could certainly not happen in Germany. As it turned out, the moment war began the 'good' Germans hastily dried their tears and got down to business.

The idea that the Germans were more aggressive in the early years of the twentieth century than other peoples was sometimes discounted in later years because it was claimed that there are no 'scientific' (i.e. biological) grounds for asserting that any national group is more aggressive than any other, or indeed for asserting that such distinctions as race or nation 'really' exist at all. But to try to study national characteristics by reference to biology is to appeal to the wrong science. National character is the product not of biology but of history; chromosomes have nothing to do with it. The Germans were unaggressive before the creation of Bismarck's Reich because they had no history of aggression behind them and no state machinery through which to make aggression effective. But by 1914 they had the machinery, and they had as their sole historic tradition a record of a successful exercise of power unparalleled in the records of European civilization. With no resources other than a relatively small army directed by his own resolute will, Bismarck had created his artificial Empire in defiance of all reasonable calculation. Neither in economic nor military strength, nor in population, had Prussia or the North German Confederation been notably superior either to Austria or to France in the 1860's. Yet the miracle had been wrought, by a few brief decisive strokes that had changed the course of destiny. Blinded by its success and flattered by its sole author, who told them that this was the German Empire of their dreams when all it was was Bismarck's Empire, the Germans appropriated the miracle to themselves as if they had wrought it through their own efforts, when the truth was that Bismarck had wrought it upon them and in spite of them. Henceforth, what had been the triumph of Bismarck's will became the triumph of the German will; and that this German will to power was irresistible became the fundamental myth of the German people, the ground which nourished all their thinking as a nation. The myth of swift, world-defying success was the more compelling because it was their only myth. It was the only German history there was. Into the history of every other nation had been written the record of defeats as well as victories, of hesitancy as well as adventurousness, of disasters as well as triumphs. This was true even of the history of Prussia, as Bismarck never forgot; but it was not true of Bismarck's Reich. Its history was only of success and therefore its national character could think only in terms of success, achieved easily and swiftly by an irresistible display of force, sometimes by the mere threat of force.

Finally, the historical tradition of the Reich knew no principle other than that of the exercise of power for its own sake. The very phrases *Weltpolitik* and *Flottenpolitik* reveal in their purposelessness that the Reich had no aim but to be powerful for the sake of being powerful. To have an aim implies a readiness not merely to take action but also to limit action to what is essential to the achievement of the aim. To have a principle necessarily involves the exercise of restraint whenever action threatens to contradict the principle. Thus, all the other powers could point to specific ambitions which they would like to satisfy. France could point to Alsace-Lorraine; Russia could point to Constantinople; England to the defence of the seas and her empire; Austria-Hungary to the destruction of Serbia. But nothing could satisfy the Germans, because they had no aims to satisfy; and nothing could satisfy the principles Germany stood for, since Germany did not stand for any. Thus diplomacy could not settle Germany's problems, because there were no problems that could be solved. There was only blind incoherent force, with which nobody could negotiate because it had no co-ordinating brain or directing intelligence. The Germans stampeded into the war, the mindless and purposeless victims of their own monstrous history.

Only against the background of a fundamental aimlessness of policy in Germany should events in Europe from 1912 to 1914 be studied. For even at this late date though the general situation made war probable, it did not make it inevitable. This is shown by the circumstance that though the Sarajevo murder led to war, the much more prolonged and complicated problems arising out of the Balkan Wars did not. The assassination of the Archduke Ferdinand implied no greater threat to the Austrian position in the Balkans than the launching of the Balkan Wars by Russia and the subsequent victories of the Balkan League. Sazonov, the Russian Foreign Minister, made the same sort of mistake that Izvolsky had made. Izvolsky had precipitated Aehrenthal into the Bosnian annexation by his own action in raising the matter of the Straits, and thereafter had wailed his way round Europe complaining bitterly that Aehrenthal had tricked him. Sazonov precipitated the Balkan Wars by patronizing the Serbo-Bulgarian treaty which started it all; and was then horrified to discover that by reconciling the pro-Austrian Bulgars with the pro-Russian Serbs he had not increased Russian influence, but had let loose against the Turks the full furies of Serb and Bulgarian nationalism. He found also that he had let loose a flood of Pan-Slav sentiment in Russia so strong that he had the very greatest difficulty in controlling it. As the Balkan Wars developed, he found himself, entirely through his own fault, as near to a Russian war against Austria-Hungary as Izvolsky had been. In the clash of petty nationalisms produced first by the Balkan League's successes and then by its internal struggle between Serbs and Bulgars, Russia found inevitably that Austria's idea of a solution was the precise opposite of

THE BALKANS, 1877–1914
RUSSIA
Braila
Belgrade
ROMANIA
Bucharest
BOSNIA
Sarajevo
HERZE-GOVINA
SERBIA
Nish
Danube
Silistria
Rustchuk
Magnalia
Plevna
BULGARIA
Varna
BLACK SEA
ADRIATIC
MONTENEGRO
Cettinje
Sofia
Burgas
EASTERN ROUMELIA
Philippopolis
Scutari
ALBANIA
MACEDONIA
Midia
Adrianople
Salonika
GREECE
Boundaries:
Proposed by Treaty of San Stefano, 1877
Congress of Berlin, 1878
After the Balkan Wars (Treaty of Bucharest)

Russia's. Russia wanted the maximum for Serbia and the minimum for Bulgaria. Austria wanted the reverse. Berchtold wanted a big Bulgaria for future use against the Serbs; he wanted Serbia kept from the Adriatic, and Montenegro deprived of Scutari; and he wanted Albania erected into a sizeable Austrian client-state on the Adriatic as a further counterbalance to both Serbs and Montenegrins. And although the defeat of Bulgaria by the other Balkan powers was a blow to Austrian policy, on all the other points the Russians gave way. Almost the last event in the story was an Austrian ultimatum to Serbia to evacuate territory allocated to Albania. Sazonov protested; but there was no question of going to war about it.

The steady policy of repentant retraction pursued by Sazonov was matched by the temperate methods of Berchtold. He was persistent, and he got what he wanted; but there was an air of measured statesmanship in his behaviour that in this period of hysteria and blundering is quite conspicuous. Nor, in this infinitely dangerous situation did the alliance system work at all in the way its mere existence would suggest as inevitable. The French were annoyed with the Russians, giving them little support. Grey worked with a kind of passionate patience to be resolutely fair-minded. His behaviour was something of a diplomatic caricature of the English sporting gentleman. When in doubt at the London Conference he nearly always gave the decision in favour of the opposing side, as if he were a particularly decent umpire at a cricket match. More remarkable still, Bethman-Hollweg in Berlin was almost as aloof towards Berchtold as Grey was towards Sazonov. Even though the Kaiser expressed the opinion that he would fight a world war for the mere sake of Austria's prestige and that the Slavs were 'born to serve', he also showed great impatience with Berchtold's anxieties on behalf of Bulgaria. Berchtold complained that the Germans were more ready to urge compromise on him than to offer concrete help.

Thus in the face of the gravest problems in international affairs since 1877, the Powers, as late as 1913, could still behave intelligently. Perhaps one clue is not simply that the Germans were 'not ready' for war but that they were not themselves directly concerned, as they had been in the two Moroccan crises, and could more easily avoid blinding themselves with considerations of German prestige. Another was the differences of character between Bethman-Hollweg and Bülow and between Aehrenthal and Berchtold. These may explain why there was not, as in 1909, a German ultimatum to Russia, and why the relatively amiable Berchtold did not try to cut the figure Aehrenthal was trying to cut in 1908.

Certainly, the difference in diplomatic reaction when the Sarajevo affair arose is so great that it is difficult to believe that Bethman-Hollweg, Berchtold and Sazonov were also the men who had handled the Balkan Wars. The chief cause of the difference is very probably that the German general staff had decided, first that a war was inevitable, and second that 1914 was the last year in which they could start this inevitable war with a reasonable chance of winning it quickly. The manpower of the Reich was not adequate for a long war: the financial system was not geared to sustain a protraction of the period of preparation for war, and indeed only made sense on the basis that the war would start very soon after 1913 and be won very soon after it had started. The appropriateness of the year 1914 for the opening of the campaign can hardly have been excluded from the various German-Austrian official meetings which took place at the end of 1913 and in the early months of 1914. Berchtold had certainly been told by the Kaiser that Austria could rely on Germany absolutely; and it was clear also that, by now, William would no longer expect to be tolerated by the German soldiers if he made any moves for peace.

Before taking refuge in blaming the German and Austrian chiefs of staff for the war it is as well to consider two points. The first is, what had convinced them that the war was 'inevitable'; the second is, what had led to their exercising so much control of the situation that everything was subordinate to their view that war was expedient solely because it was *militarily* expedient. Both circumstances must clearly be regarded as the outcome of the sins of omission and commission of the politicians and diplomats. It is always the business of soldiers to plan wars and to say whether or not their military resources are such as to make a war at any given date a feasible proposition. That is what soldiers are for; and in saying in 1913 that a war could only be won if it were started fairly soon, the German soldiers were merely doing their duty. 'Success alone justifies war,' Moltke is reported to have said in 1913, and as the technical proposition of a professional soldier it is sensible enough. It is wrong to blame the German general staff for wanting war in 1914; the blame must be attributed to those who, in the face of this information, had no idea of doing anything except to act upon it. It was the German and Austrian political systems, and the second-rate minds that operated and acquiesced in those systems that were responsible for the war, not the general staffs.

As for the widespread view that war was inevitable, that was due also to the past blunders of the politicians and to the easy assumption that those blunders could never be rectified or their dangerous consequences postponed. Yet the handling of the Balkan Wars had proved the opposite less than twelve months before August 1914. The whole conception of inevitability in human affairs is often no more than a confession of political incompetence. It implies that tendencies, themselves created by human beings, cannot be checked, diverted, or even reversed by human beings. The history of the nineteenth century contains many examples of how 'inevitable' developments can be successfully resisted for a very long time. The break-up of the Habsburg Empire and the triumph of the Revolution had both been regarded as inevitable by Metternich; but neither inevitability had occurred by 1900. In 1900 a war between England and the French and Russians had seemed inevitable; but by 1914 they were allies together. The careers of Palmerston, Metternich, Cavour, Garibaldi and Bismarck all proved that various forms of greatness could triumph over inevitabilities. What made war inevitable in 1914 was a failure of human intelligence, human courage, and human good will. The men of 1914 let the war happen not because it was inevitable but because they could not think of anything better to do.

Those who gave up most completely were Berchtold and Bethman-Hollweg. Berchtold's attitude was one of political helplessness disguised as resolute defence of Austria's national interests. The Dual Monarchy had, since the defection of Roumania to the Triple Entente at the end of 1913, been faced with the menace of a Great Serbia, directed at Austrian control of Bosnia, Dalmatia and Croatia-Slavonia, and the menace of a Great Roumania directed at Transylvania on the east. It was as if, in 1899, the English had been faced by the two Boer Republics, not two continents away but as close as the mountains of Wales and the lowlands of Scotland; and it was a danger to the Dual Monarchy whose seriousness must not be minimized. Serbian nationalism was a savage thing, born of centuries of oppression, and therefore ugly with accumulated hatred and suppressed ambitions. The assassination at Sarajevo was its brutal consequence; and that the Dual Monarchy had the right to take strong action is sometimes overlooked in the understandable hurry to condemn the action that was in fact taken. Nor does the view that the Serbs inside the Dual Monarchy had a right, if they so wished, to join with the free Serbs to form a Great Serb state justify an assumption that the first duty of the Dual Monarchy was to give its Slav provinces away. But the fundamental character of the problem, as a clash of German against Slav, race against race, demanded that it be handled with superlative delicacy and restraint. In failing to display either quality, the Dual Monarchy was repeating, in more explosive circumstances, the error of the British towards the Boers, and rehearsing the later errors of European powers in general when faced with the strident and often savage nationalism of races regarded by them as backward or inferior. No amount of righteous anger about their crime in plunging Europe into war should obscure the difficulty of the Dual Monarchy's position in 1914.

Yet the choice was not between survival by destroying Serbia or committing suicide through failing to do so. To attempt to destroy Serbia was bound to mean war; and this was the speediest of all methods of committing suicide that the Dual Monarchy had open to it. The choice in 1914 was between moderation and death; and death not only for the Dual Monarchy but for the European order as well. Berchtold opted for death. His pretence that the war ought to be confined to Austria-Hungary and Serbia was a patent fraud, for in fact he acted only because he knew he was sure of German support. Such support could mean only that the war became European.

German responsibility is therefore basic. Without the expressed belief of the German soldiers that if a general war came they would win it and win it quickly, Austria would have had to act with Europe and not in defiance of it, and Berchtold would not have been able to make his fatal choice. Divorced from the basic proposition that a war was welcome, German and Austrian behaviour does not in fact make sense.

Bethman-Hollweg made no attempt to intervene to restrain the Austrians until it was too late: and to try to restrain the Austrians when he could not even constrain his own soldiers was a waste of time. Furthermore, his anxiety in proposing moderation to Austria was not so much to avoid the war as to avoid the appearance of having started it. Once the Russians had mobilized, this problem was solved for him. Russia had mobilized; therefore the Germans were free from the charge of being 'the real authors of war' since it was clearly Russia who was turning an Austro-Serb conflict into European war. Yet Bethman-Hollweg was castigating the Russians for secret military preparations against Austria when in fact the whole crisis arose from secret military preparations by Germany to support the Dual Monarchy in all circumstances.

Absolved from any necessity to take further steps worthy of a statesman on his eastern flank, Bethman-Hollweg then proceeded, not as a diplomatic but purely as a military precaution and as a propaganda device, to seek British neutrality. Grey's notorious sense of principle would thus be harnessed to the German campaign to prove that this was a just and necessary war. Yet Bethman-Hollweg's methods when trying to bargain the British into acquiescence in the German war plan were as frivolous as they were unscrupulous. No promises were made about Belgium, and, almost laughably, it was suggested that when victory was won, English concern for France as a European power would be respected by an undertaking that Germany would content herself with annexing the French colonial empire. Such a suggestion in itself was almost an adequate justification for British participation in the war. The proposal was a threat to the British almost as serious as the invasion of Belgium. Yet this programme was seriously represented as an attempt to preserve English friendship. The defence of German action which Bethman-Hollweg presented to the Reichstag on August 4 makes the matter clearer still. It amounted to one more appeal to the historic German myth of Realpolitik. We are violating international law, but necessity knows no law. He omitted to insert the word 'German' before the word 'necessity'; but the context shows it was intended to be understood. Germany's necessity knew no law. It was the one and only article in the historical dogma of the Bismarckian Reich: and Bethman-Hollweg, the sincere and gentlemanly lover of peace, discovered in the crisis that that was all he believed in too.

Since German mobilization was ordered before Berlin had news of Russia's similar action, the view that Russian mobilization was a deciding factor in making the war general does not seem a very sound one. Moreover, Russia had been told by the Germans that even preparatory military action would be followed by a German mobilization. Russian inaction in 1914 could only be demanded on the assumption that Russia ought always to submit to having its policy dictated to it by Berlin and Vienna. It may be that Russian support of Serbia was a bad thing; but it can hardly be counted in the scales against German support of the Dual Monarchy. The Russian attitude was the reasonable one that an Austrian invasion of Serbia could not be regarded as a punitive expedition against an inferior race of savage mountain tribesmen which was nobody else's business but Vienna's. In mobilizing to insist that Serbs had as much right to an independent existence as Germans had, Russia could be represented as acting in defence not merely of Russian prestige and of Pan-Slavism, but of elementary human principles. There was after all no evidence that Russia was herself using Serbia to threaten the existence of the Dual Monarchy.

The Austrian negotiations with Russia on the matter were dishonest. Berchtold had in mind, as the Austrian war aim, the partition of Serbia among the other Balkan states, with perhaps annexation of some parts of it to the Dual Monarchy. Yet the Austrian ambassador was instructed to say in St Petersburg that there was no intention to infringe Serbian sovereignty. This is a fair indication that the Austrians expected war with the Russians and were merely trying to fool them into leaving their mobilization until it was too late.

Grey has been criticized on two counts. Russia believed that Austria could have been deterred by an early announcement of a British intention to intervene; and it is suggested that this would have made it possible for him to advise Russia to postpone her mobilization. The brief answer is that English public opinion made it impossible for Grey to make such a statement of England's intentions. It is also unlikely that Austria would have been any more deterred by such an announcement than the Germans, who fully expected British intervention. After all, the attitude of the Austrians had all along been, 'What can the British do to us?' And to advise Russia to postpone their mobilization would have been to ask the Russians to fall into the German trap, since it was regarded as an urgent military necessity in Berlin that the Russians must not be given time to mobilize first. There was little that Grey could do in 1914 to save the peace, because the Germans would not let him.

Even if public opinion had been in favour of it, it is unlikely that Grey himself would ever have formed an alliance with Russia, any more than with France, and it would have made no difference in 1914 had such an alliance existed. The behaviour of the Germans had eliminated all the risks that the English ran by their association with France and Russia, and substituted the overriding danger of a German attempt at the swift and irreversible acquisition of world power. The very danger that the British had sought to eliminate from 1898 onwards had been recreated—by the Germans. This danger had been that a combined Franco-Russian attack on their empire would be beyond England's capacity to resist. But a German victory, if achieved with the speed intended by the Germans, would have involved Germany's acquisition of the French navy and the French Empire, and German domination of western Europe and its ocean approaches. A victory over Russia would have opened the Near and Far East to unchallengeable German exploitation. The outbreak of war in 1914 carried the threat that by the end of 1915 German power could look forward confidently to the mobilization in Europe, Africa and Asia, of the material resources of both France and Russia for an attack on the United Kingdom and the British Empire which they could not hope to resist. The British were in the end drawn into the war not because of their *entente* with France and Russia; nor would they have been drawn into it by the mere fact of an alliance with them had such existed. They were drawn in, in purely British interests, by the inescapable fact of the German will to power.

The dilatoriness of the British cabinet in the face of the situation is one of the most extraordinary features of the story of the last weeks of peace. Its almost academic unawareness of the realities of the crisis forms a strange contrast to the clear-cut ruthlessness with which minds were made up elsewhere. Perhaps the most bizarre feature of all was a remark made by Lloyd George, who seriously suggested that England and Italy should deal with the problem by both being neutral and thus, 'as it were, pairing with each other'; he might have been speaking of a struggle as artificial and as civilian as the clash between Liberals and Conservatives about the House of Lords. The cabinet explored the idea of neutrality to the furthest limit of reminding themselves that the Treaty of London of 1839 did not imply automatic action to defend Belgian neutrality in all circumstances. Indeed, the matter was not even discussed until July 30, and Lloyd George's later assertion that if it had been, the cabinet would have at once agreed to defend Belgium is apparently unsupported by the recollections of others. Also unsupported by the evidence is the idea that it would have made any difference. The opportunity to preserve peace was denied Grey in 1914; all he could do was to try to keep the cabinet from collapsing so that a German victory was not ensured by a paralysis of government in London during the war's first critical days and weeks. In that task he succeeded; and to such an extent that on August 3 even Lloyd George's political education had at last advanced to the point where he could believe that not only was Belgium a gallant little nation like Wales, but so also was Serbia. One step behind even Lloyd George, opinion in England was prevented by its sentimental belief in the fundamental goodness of Germans and the fundamental badness of Frenchmen and Russians from grasping until the very last moment that there was any problem at all. Only by being directed to the Belgian issue could they be made to understand what was at stake; just as in 1701 the English could be persuaded that Louis XIV's Spanish policy was a threat to them only when they had been told that he had recognized the Old Pretender as James III.

It has been suggested since 1945 that there was not only a moral but also a political error in the English association with Russia in 1914. The moral view is based on the suggestion that association with Czarist Russia made nonsense of the claim of the English that the *Entente* was fighting for freedom or for democracy. Yet neither freedom nor democracy would have been served by allowing any part of Russia to fall under German control; and although it is possible to forgive Englishmen for failing to realize this in 1914, it is difficult to condone such obtuseness after 1945. As for the political objection, this too must perforce be rejected. There were grave risks to both England and Europe in associating Russia with a war against Germany, since if the *Entente* won, Russia might well have reached in 1919 that position she held in 1945, with the additional advantage of possessing Constantinople, promised her by a wartime treaty. It was the Bolshevik revolution, an event outside the calculations of the diplomats, that prevented this particular consequence of British diplomacy from arising in 1919. But the difficulty, once again, is that of pointing to an alternative policy superior to that actually pursued. A balance of power in central and eastern Europe between Germans and Slavs was unquestionably a highly desirable aim; but a German victory would have destroyed it at least as completely as an allied victory in which Czarist Russia survived to participate.

It is visionary to suppose that England was somehow free to let the Germans and the Russians fight it out among themselves to a stalemate, at which point England would enter the field as an arbiter imposing on equally exhausted combatants a solution which preserved a balance between them. To think this is to commit precisely the same error of over-subtle calculation based on ignorance of the facts which Napoleon III is so fiercely criticized for having committed when he decided to be neutral in the Seven Weeks War. In the first place, Germany would not, given the technical competence of her staff, plunge into an all-out war with Russia unless she were sure of victory; and alliances or no alliances, that war would not be undertaken unless Germany was first sure of destroying the French. The grim facts of life in 1914, as in the 1930's, were that any clever scheme for diverting Germany into a life and death struggle with Russia required first of all the elimination of France an an effective great power. The Franco-Russian alliances of 1890 and 1935 were a simple recognition of this elementary fact; and the policy of Germany in 1914 and from 1939 to 1941 is a recognition of it also. In 1914 France was saved in the first place because there was an alliance with Russia; and the absence of such an alliance in 1940 is a sufficient explanation of the French defeat in that year. The fact that the maintenance of France as a great power was vital to British security, if not to British existence, was the essential justification of an alliance with Russia, whatever its potential dangers. It was a high price to have to pay; and it was only by what was in a sense a stroke of luck that the bill was not presented to Lloyd George and Wilson in 1919 but to Churchill and Roosevelt in 1945. But in the end all that the objection to the link with Russia amounts to is an assertion that a balance of power between Germany and Russia existed in 1914 and could not be expected to survive a war. Avoidance of war was certainly a supreme British interest; but it is extremely difficult to see what more the British could have done to avoid war, and impossible to assert that their interests would have been better served by neutrality than by participation.

XV

THROUGH WAR TO PEACE 1914–1920

THE general expectation in Europe in 1914 was that the war would, like the wars of 1859, 1866 and 1870, be over quickly. Those wars could be adequately summed up in terms of decisive battles—Magenta and Solferino, Sadowa and Sedan. There was, it is true, a decisive battle in 1914, the battle of the Marne; but the decision there was that the war would be prolonged. Instead of the expected swift surgical operation, Europe had to face a slow bleeding to death.

The protraction of the war posed for the *entente* powers the associated problems of alliances and war aims, for the two were closely connected until the very end of the war. Much was involved in the espousal of the German cause by Turkey. It helped to produce the allied promise that Russia should have Constantinople; this in turn led naturally to Anglo-French plans for the partition of the rest of the Turkish Empire, and this, not unnaturally, gave colour later on to the view of the war as one fought for the sake of '*entente* imperialism'. It helped also to produce the embarrassing adherence of Italy to the allied side: for if Russia was to grope forward towards the Mediterranean, Italy was needed as a counter. The intervention of Italy gave the war an anti-Habsburg character, which strictly it lacked otherwise, since Italy alone of the allies had territorial claims on the Dual Monarchy. Italian ambitions in this direction also created Italo-Serb rivalry for the Adriatic coast, and by reaction stimulated into new life the larger dreams of a South Slav kingdom which included not only Serbia but the Croat and

Slovene provinces in the Habsburg Empire. The entry of Roumania into the war in 1916 similarly helped to make the dismemberment of the Habsburg Empire a war aim, since the Roumanians' reward was, naturally enough, to be Transylvania. This process of dismemberment, once envisaged, could, in the event of allied victory, hardly be resisted or prevented from going even further. Thus, the partition of the Turkish and the Habsburg empires arose, not out of the causes of the war or out of the aims of the Great Powers who launched it, but out of their wartime diplomacy. The lesser allies of England, France and Russia, though of little military use to them, had therefore a great influence on the shaping of the peace; the fact helps to explain how slow the English and the French were to admit that the destruction of Austria-Hungary was a chief war aim. From their point of view it was not a chief war aim: it was something to which they found themselves committed in spite of themselves and about which English and French governments remained conspicuously unenthusiastic long after it had actually come to pass. It showed a sound instinct on the part of the Emperor Karl that he should try to save the Habsburg Monarchy from ruin by the negotiations for a separate peace in 1917. Doomed though the negotiations were, they registered, both in their initiation and in the eagerness with which the allies at first received them, facts that by then had been almost forgotten. Karl had entered upon an inheritance doomed by the desires and follies of men other than the statesmen of France and England.

The real problem, however, was Germany, and here the correct historical analogy is not with the wars of Bismarck, but with the Crimean War. Fought largely because Russia was too powerful, the Crimean War produced no permanently decisive result because the allies were not strong enough decisively to reduce Russia's power by military means, and too disunited after the war to keep it for long in check by diplomacy. In a similar way, the real grievance of the allied powers against the German Reich was that it had too much power and had used that power recklessly. Yet they found themselves unable to prevent a great extension of German territorial control taking place as soon as the war began. Undefeated though the allies were, Germany was soon impregnably in control of the whole of the centre of Europe from the North Sea to the Black Sea.

There could be no peace for the allies while the Germans held so much; on the other hand there could be no victory for the Germans while the allied armies were still in being. The deadlock was thus not only military; it was also diplomatic. There could be no compromise peace, because even if the Germans offered to withdraw from the occupied territories (and they never offered even that in full) this would still provide no answer to the problem of allied security. What Germany had done with her 1914 resources she could presumably do again, even if reduced back to those limits. Therefore the circumstances of the case compelled the allies to look for much more than merely the restoration of Belgium, for instance. On the west it would be impossible for the French to believe in a victory that did not give them Alsace-Lorraine, since the loss of those provinces was the essential symbol of French defeat. On the east, wartime diplomacy again affected policy. Once the Germans chose to espouse the cause of Polish independence, the allies were bound in the end to do likewise, whether they wanted to or not. Given these considerations on the allied side, curtailment of the war by diplomacy was impossible. Only by militarily defeating them or exhausting them could the Germans hope to get the allies to make peace. Thus, suggestions for a compromise peace on the allied side tended to arise whenever the prevailing impression was of the impossibility of beating the Germans, never because the allies were in sight of a diplomatic settlement that would really satisfy them. Moreover, the Germans saw such suggestions, not as the prelude to a compromise, but as an attempt to stave off imminent allied defeat. They therefore put on such suggestions the purely military interpretation that final victory was within reach. The very absence of concrete German aims and of effective political direction in Berlin aggravated the deadlock. There being nothing specific the Germans wanted there was nothing specific that could satisfy them. Between their demand for victory and the allies' demand for security, compromise was impossible.

German victory was near enough in 1917, with the collapse of the Russians and the breakdown of army morale in France. Once again, as so often before, the Germans wrecked their cause by an initiative of their own. The launching of the submarine campaign at once made the United States a potential participant, and moreover one with whom only the allies would negotiate seriously, because they so badly needed United States assistance. The Germans calculated that the war would be over before the United States could give effective help, just as they had calculated that it would be over in 1914 before the British could give effective help. Accordingly the Germans shocked the United States in December 1916 by their views on what would constitute suitable peace terms; but they did not mind being shocking. The allies were more circumspect; and it was out of the need to satisfy the greatest of their associates that they were brought to the point of putting together a coherent set of war aims in January 1917. In a very real sense these aims constituted a cautious summary of their past promises to their European allies and to one another, with suitable additions and modifications to suit the known preconceptions of the American President.

From January 1917 until the late spring of 1918, the allies and President Wilson between them proceeded to dangle before the eyes of a world struggling in the toils of a seemingly endless war the intoxicating prospect of a heaven on earth at the end of it all. Wilson was inspired by that deep sense of conviction which is the unique possession of those who combine profound idealism with profounder ignorance. The British and French supported him as an act of diplomacy and public relations. It is easy to be cynical about this but the difficulty was that the allies could only get Wilson's help by uttering phrases of the sort that he himself delighted to utter. In addition, people had the right to expect a better world as a result of their suffering, and the statesmen had a moral duty to try to give it to them. The trouble was that Wilson's exalted unawareness of realities was not matched by serious statesmanship among the French and the English. Clemenceau merely wanted revenge, and Lloyd George, though he understood people with intuitive genius, understood foreign affairs hardly at all, and was not much better informed about Europe than Wilson. A statesmanlike synthesis between idealism and the facts of the European situation was therefore not forthcoming, and it is perhaps not too harsh to say that diplomatic history from 1918 to 1920 is concerned with a chaos compounded of ignorance and smooth opportunism. The English badly wanted to moderate Wilson's idealism; but what they did seems to have been to support it in public, while manœuvring against it in secret. The result was to discredit the peace settlement, not because its terms were bad, but because they failed to conform to a series of wildly exaggerated promises that ought never to have been made.

Wilson viewed the war in much the same way as the left wing in England had viewed it in 1914 and was again beginning to view it under the influence of the heady slogans of the Russian Revolution. As far as Wilson was concerned, Germany's crime was adequately defined as that of having violated the territory of small nations; and all that the war was for was the restoration of these small nations to their former status. There was nothing greatly wrong with the state system in Europe in 1914 as such; and Wilson would have liked it restored with only minor changes. The future would be looked after by removing what were considered to be the 'real' causes of war. Among these were Prussian militarism, the abolition of which would at once transform Germany into a liberal and pacific democracy; secret treaties, regardless of the fact that few important treaties were really very secret and that no treaty, secret or otherwise, was invoked by any of the contestants in 1914; and—very confusingly indeed since they could hardly exist together—the principle of the balance of power and something dramatically called 'international anarchy'. All were to be abolished by general disarmament, beginning with the Germans, and by the creation of a League of Nations which, by waving the fairy wand of universal brotherhood among nations, would enable everyone to live happily ever afterwards.

In view of this it was necessary, in order to secure Wilson's co-operation, to adopt a tone of sweetest reasonableness. Thus, in January 1918, Lloyd George, so adept at echoing the views of others, declared:

> 'We are not fighting a war of aggression against the German people. . . . Nor are we fighting to destroy Austria-Hungary. . . . Nor did we enter this war merely to alter or destroy the Imperial constitution of Germany. . . . Our point of view is that the adoption of a really democratic constitution would make it easier for us to conclude a broad democratic peace with her. But after all that is a question for the Germans themselves to decide.'

Three days later, echo answered him, in Wilson's speech announcing the Fourteen Points and containing the following:

> 'We have no jealousy of German greatness. . . . We do not wish to injure her or block in any way her legitimate influence or power. . . .

Neither do we presume to suggest to her any alterations or modifications of her institutions.'

The trouble with this amiable nonsense was that it impressed itself on the minds of everybody at the time except the Germans. The Germans ignored it; and only when they were at last faced with the prospect of total defeat did they suddenly proclaim that they had been offered a 'just' peace which would not injure their greatness. The point was that by the end of 1918 the Germans had forfeited any right to appeal to these principles, because to all intents and purposes they had rejected the Fourteen Points. They had preferred instead to answer them with an all-out drive for total victory. The German reply to the Fourteen Points was perfectly clear. It consisted of the treaty of Brest-Litovsk with Russia and that of Bucharest with Roumania. These, coming hard on the heels of Wilson's Fourteen Points and Four Principles, proved beyond doubt that the German idea of 'a peace of understanding and conciliation' involved unlimited annexation. The German Reich was not, after all, an organization like other state organizations in Europe. It was a ruthless machine for subjugation and conquest. The German Reich regarded the rest of Europe as populated by racial inferiors, and its aim was the reduction of the other states of Europe to the condition of colonial dependencies.

Wilson's reaction was clear enough, but ignored in Germany and barely noticed even in the history books. In April 1918 he said:

> 'I am ready to discuss a fair and just and honest peace at any time. . . . But the answer when I proposed such a peace [i.e. in January 1918] came from the German commanders in Russia and I cannot mistake the meaning of the answer. I accept the challenge. . . . Germany has once more said that force and force alone shall decide whether justice and peace shall reign in the affairs of men.'

Similarly the British also produced a sharp reminder on this point in October 1918 when the Germans, in asking for an armistice, stated that they accepted Wilson's January 1918 programme 'as a basis for peace negotiations'. The British comment ran:

'. . . the pronouncements of President Wilson were a statement of attitude made before the Brest-Litovsk Treaty [and] the enforcement of the peace of Bucharest on Roumania. . . . They cannot, therefore, be understood as a full recitation of the conditions of peace.'

Significant of the actual state of mind in allied circles at the time is that Lloyd George notes, concerning a British cabinet meeting on October 24th 1918:

'Mr Bonar Law expressed his pleasure that President Wilson had been firm enough, when it came to the point, to insist on what practically amounted to unconditional surrender.'

Thus the arrogant self-confidence and ruthlessness of the Germans in their dealings with defeated Russia and Roumania, and their repeated insistence that the only peace they were interested in was one which gathered the fruits of victory into their own barns, had knocked most of the generosity out of the heads of allied statesmen long before the Paris conference opened. Both Wilson and the British were now convinced that to achieve a 'peace without victory' was, as far as Germany was concerned, out of the question. Even before the armistice the allies had adopted the view that the Fourteen Points were to be open to modification only in a sense favourable to themselves and not at all in a sense favourable to the Germans. The way was therefore clear for Clemenceau when the conference opened. The purpose of the settlement was not at all to try to be fair and just to the Germans, but to impose drastic penalties upon them.

Unfortunately, whereas Wilson's various idealistic pronouncements had received world-wide publicity, the modifications of them decided upon between April and October 1918 had not. Worse still, nothing could deter Wilson from continuing all through the year to utter noble-sounding phrases which implied that the conference would be guided solely by the most exalted precepts. 'No peace,' he announced as late as September 27th 1918, 'shall be obtained by any kind of compromise or abatement of the principles we have avowed.' Wilson's historical studies can have taught him but little if he could think in terms like that. The truth was that Wilson suffered from much the same sort of moral megalomania as that which afflicted Alexander I in 1815 and Frederick William IV between 1840 and 1848. Elevated and sonorous phrases were propounded by all of them because such phrases were currently popular and because they were men intoxicated by a sense of their own righteousness and by the opportunity they imagined to be theirs to become the saviours of the world. The label 'demagogue' ought not to be restricted to those who, regardless of consequences, appeal to the lowest in the human mind. It ought to be applied sometimes to men like Wilson, who appeal to the highest in men; for to tell humanity that peace and justice are about to be achieved without 'any kind of compromise or abatement' is to practise the worst of all forms of deceit.

Wilson made a further resolution, induced by Brest-Litovsk, to strengthen his opinion that the Hohenzollerns must go, and with them, the Prussian 'militarists': Germany must become a democracy. Accordingly, he virtually refused to treat with the German Imperial Government. He would demand 'not peace negotiations but surrender' if he had to deal 'with the military masters and monarchical autocrats' of Germany, and would sign only with 'the veritable representatives of the German people'.

This was a blunder. It created the entirely false impression among the Germans that if they overthrew the Hohenzollerns and manufactured democratic institutions they would escape the consequences of defeat. The facts are that the British, and the Americans by now, had already decided on a severe peace, which would not be limited by the Fourteen Points; and they were to be given no chance by the French to go back on that sensible decision. But the Germans did not know this; nor, it seems, did public opinion with the disastrous result that the peace treaty could, not without justice, be regarded as having been brought about by a piece of shameful deceit on the part of the allies.

What made this all the more ironical was the fact that the real act of deceit came from the Germans themselves. The German Revolution of 1918, out of which the Weimar Republic emerged, was an attempt to bamboozle the British and Americans into granting Germany a lenient peace treaty, while at the same time keeping the German army intact, if not in its organization, at the least in its reputation.

Ludendorff asked for an armistice solely to preserve the German army. He had Prince Max of Baden and a so-called Liberal cabinet installed in Berlin solely to persuade the allies that Germany now had fully representative institutions, and he badgered Prince Max to ask for an armistice as soon as possible. Unconvinced by the reality of Germany's conversion, and over-sensitive at the continuance of William II as Emperor, Wilson pronounced himself dissatisfied. So after safeguarding the future by demanding a renewal of the war, Ludendorff went. Then, since the Kaiser was of no further use either to the army as a peace negotiator, or to the country as a symbol of success, he went too. He was dismissed in circumstances not dissimilar to those surrounding the dismissal of Metternich in 1848: as Metternich was sacrificed to the revolutionaries of Vienna, so the Kaiser was sacrificed to the Spartacists of Berlin. In both cases the idea was to persuade the mob that they had got what they wanted. In 1918 however, the idea was also to persuade the allies that they had got what they wanted, a genuine democratic Germany. The Spartacists were not fooled, but in the long run the allies were. For the republic that emerged was designed to keep power out of the hands of the revolutionaries and pacifists, and it was governed by much the same people who had figured in the government of Prince Max; and so far from being opposed to the High Command these men at once sought an alliance with it for the purpose of suppressing the revolutionaries.

The consequence of all this muddle was that only the German army leadership emerged intact from it. The idea that because the Imperial autocrats and militarists started the war it was impossible to sign a peace treaty with them was supremely illogical. They, one would have thought, were just the people with whom it should have been signed. Versailles should have been signed by plenipotentiaries representing Ludendorff rather than by shadow creatures representing Ebert, who stood for nothing real in Germany at all. For, obscured by these shadowy creatures, the army leaders survived, undefeated in the hour of defeat, and unsullied by the slightest association with the document that registered that defeat.

Moreover—and the point is vital—so little had been changed by the absurd policy of trying to compel the Germans to be democratic by allied fiat that it was nothing but the sheer lack of an army to fight with that prevented the Germans from resuming the war as soon as the treaty terms were presented to them. The army leaders meanwhile remained the real force behind the scenes in Germany and the real representatives of German opinion. They could now say, and not without a show of truth, that they had been tricked, if not into defeat, at any rate into the Treaty of Versailles.

Thus the failure of the allies to insist on the real nature of the German menace until after Wilson had issued his Fourteen Points was a major disaster. For while the Fourteen Points and Four Principles and Wilson's subsequent high-sounding elaborations of them were disseminated far and wide, the allied recovery of a sense of realities after Brest-Litovsk was not. This was to lead to that undermining of their faith in their own cause which almost led to England and France losing the Second World War before it had started. Worse still, the misguided attempt to make the Germans democrats by compulsion created in the Germans the impression that they could escape the consequences of their responsibility for the war, and of their defeat. They who in the event of victory would have conceded it to nobody were themselves to be treated with justice: and the existence of the Fourteen Points enabled them to go on insisting subsequently that they 'ought' to have had justice and that they were an innocent people deceived by the allies into laying down arms on terms which the allies had no intention of carrying out. So it came to be accepted that the Germans were in a sad plight, not because they had started and then lost a war, but because the wicked allies had cheated them in 1918.

The impression was reinforced by the decision to exclude the Germans from the negotiation of the treaty terms. Their presence would have greatly prolonged those negotiations; but the presentation of the terms in the form of what amounted to a comprehensive ultimatum to a people much less capable of free choice even than the Serbs in 1914 gave the Germans yet another chance to evade the full realization of the fact that they had lost the war. It might still have been possible to bring it home to them if they had been compelled to admit it point by point at the conference table. Instead they could henceforth, and with a show of justification, speak of the treaty as a '*diktat*'. It was, as has been said, of paramount importance that accredited German representatives should themselves have been brought to an admission of defeat; instead, that salutary confession was never made by the Germans at all. They were foolishly allowed to go on record as helpless martyrs protesting vainly against other people's injustice, instead of as repentant criminals who freely admitted both their guilt and their acceptance of its consequences.

As it was, the German claim that the terms of Versailles could be summed up in the sentence 'L'Allemagne renonce à son existence' must be regarded as one of the bad jokes of recent history. By 1925, German steel production was twice that of Great Britain and while the latter's industrial production in that year was only ninety-two per cent of the 1914 figure the corresponding figure for Germany was 117. For a country that had renounced its existence, Germany did very well indeed in the fifteen years after 1919, despite its losses in that year and the later inflation and depression. The territorial settlement imposed on the Germans was not in fact particularly severe. The return of Alsace-Lorraine to France was inevitable and only the Germans would have expected anything else; and the other cessions to Belgium, Czechoslovakia and Denmark were not crippling. It is worth recalling that the only standard of comparison by which the Versailles treaty can be properly judged is that of the Germans' own treaty with the Russians at Brest-Litovsk. This the Germans regarded as a peace based on 'understanding and conciliation'; yet it deprived Russia of thirty-four per cent of her population, fifty-four per cent of her industrial undertakings and eighty-nine per cent of her coal mines. Nor was the cession of territory to the new Poland at all the tragedy the Germans insisted it was. While it might be good for historians in general to be a little less partisan in their treatment of the Polish problem, it is requisite that they accept as fundamental the proposition that Poles had as much right to a national existence and to the economic necessities of that existence as the Germans. This the Germans never accepted; and much sympathy was sought and obtained by them on account of the separation of East Prussia from the rest of the Reich by the Polish Corridor. But there was nothing in the least unnatural about this. It was a mere matter of geography. It was not the fault of the Poles or the allies but of the Germans themselves that East Prussia was where it was, on the further side of Poland, and it was no more contrary to justice than the fact that an Englishman who wished to travel overland to Gibraltar had to cross the territory of France and Spain. Nor was the loss of the German colonial empire a serious blow. It made far less difference to the Germans than the disappearance of their colonial empire would have made to the French; and the Germans would certainly have taken over the French colonies had the allies been defeated. Finally, there was nothing at all vindictive about either the demilitarization of the Rhineland or the fifteen-year cession of the Saar to the French.

Of all the various objections to the disarmament and reparations clauses, the most serious was that they could not be enforced. It was also a mistake to imply that German disarmament was to be connected with general disarmament. The real reason for the disarmament clauses was that it was hoped they would make Germany powerless. Instead, it was indicated that the object was to enable the other powers to disarm. This they did not do, and the fact provided more nourishment for the belligerent self-pity of the Germans. Thus the allies got nothing out of the disarmament clauses except a general reputation for hypocrisy. As for the celebrated 'war guilt' clause, inserted to justify reparations, it is difficult to see what were the value of the objections to it. It imputed 'sole' responsibility not to Germany, but to 'Germany and her allies'. Whether this was intended to mean that Germany and her allies were responsible legally, practically, or morally does not really matter. In whatever sense the word 'responsibility' is taken, to apply it to Germany and her allies was merely to state historical fact. The clause naturally stimulated a number of historians inside and outside Germany to try to prove that the war was really the fault of the French or the Russians, or Sir Edward Grey, or armament manufacturers or the balance of power and so forth; but by now there is no need to take such attempts seriously.

The problem of Austria-Hungary is often regarded as a quite separate issue from that of Germany, but was in fact inseparable from it. It has been seen that the dissolution of the Dual Monarchy was not envisaged when the war began, though wartime diplomacy made it probable: it is not even precisely specified in the Fourteen Points. It has been alleged also that but for Wilson's energetic encouragement of the principle of self-determination it might have held together. This is perhaps not only to under-estimate the strength of the Czechoslovak and Jugoslav liberation movements, but to ignore the fact that the course of the war had reduced the Bismarckian division of Germany into one state governed from Berlin and another governed from Vienna to a palpable fiction. The events of the war faced Europe with a solid German-Magyar power bloc stretching from the Baltic to the Balkans and directly controlled by Berlin. It is difficult to see how Austria-Hungary could have been preserved after 1919 and yet kept free from control by Berlin. For the simple fact was that only if Austria-Hungary was entirely freed from Berlin could it be anything other than what it had been from 1908 to 1918—a means for the maintenance of German domination throughout south-east Europe and a permanent jumping-off ground for the penetration of Turkey and Asia Minor. A German *imperium* from Berlin to Bagdad was implicit in any scheme for the maintenance of the Habsburg Monarchy after 1919; and in applying the principle of self-determination to the Slavs and the Roumanians the peace treaties did in fact create a state system which, while it lasted, prevented that *imperium* from reviving. A great Poland, a great Roumania and a great Serbia rechristened Jugoslavia, together with Czechoslovakia, effectively cut off Germany from Russia, from the Balkans and from Turkey, reduced the Magyars to impotence, and Austria to its ancient status as a German outpost amid a world of Slavs. The refusal to allow Austria, even when shorn of its non-German provinces, to unite with the German Reich called forth much sympathy among the many critics of the 1919 Settlement. Yet it was to miss the whole significance of the war to imagine that either peace or justice would have been served by making Austria a part of the Reich. Berlin's influence would then stretch directly via Vienna and (inevitably) via Budapest to the borders of Transylvania; it would have loomed over almost the entire northern frontier of Jugoslavia; and would have condemned Czechoslovakia to encirclement by its ancient German and Magyar enemies from the very day of its birth.

Seen in this light, the peace treaties of 1919 have a clear justification as an attempt to contain the German Reich by the liberation of the Slavs, and the peasants of Transylvania. The cause both of peace and justice was served in eastern Europe by the treaties; and better served than they had been for centuries. It was not the Versailles system but the success of the Germans in wrecking it in 1938 and 1939 that caused the Second World War. The real German grievance against the settlement was not that it was a '*diktat*' or that they had been cheated by President Wilson. It was chiefly that it prevented them from dominating and exploiting the valleys of the Vistula and the Danube and kept them away from the approaches to Asia Minor and the Ukraine, and because it emphatically asserted that in south-eastern Europe the Slavs had as much right to an independent existence as the Germans and Magyars.

It is easy to be cynical about the imperfections of the new state system, but it is a cynicism which relies far too much for justification on the disparity between the realities and the irresponsible demagogy of Wilson's peace programme. It is true that Czechoslovakia was a polyglot, manufactured state, that Jugoslavia was even more of a Great Serbia than Cavour's Italy had been a Great Piedmont, that Roumania was corrupt, that Austria was bankrupt, Hungary reactionary and Poland irresponsible and ruthless. It is true that most of these states contained national minorities few of whom were justly treated. But only the naïve and uninformed could have hoped for anything better. To emphasize these imperfections is to show an inability to grasp the character of the problem as great as was Wilson's inability. The imperfections of the new situation in eastern Europe were at the same time an inevitable consequence of centuries of history and a vast improvement on anything that had existed there before. Even at this date voices are still raised to declare that Austria-Hungary ought to have been maintained, but nearly always on the baseless assumption that it was a multi-national state that covered all south-east Europe with a mantle of peace and civilization. The truth is, however, that the Dual Monarchy was based on German and Magyar domination and Slav inferiority; whereas in those regions the facts pointed in the opposite direction. In the area occupied by the Habsburg Monarchy history and geography had made the Slavs the more numerous people, and the 1919 Settlement put the Germans and Magyars at long last in their rightful position as two racial minorities. It was not unusual to hear the Versailles system criticized as producing the 'Balkanization' of eastern Europe, as though this were a very bad thing. But

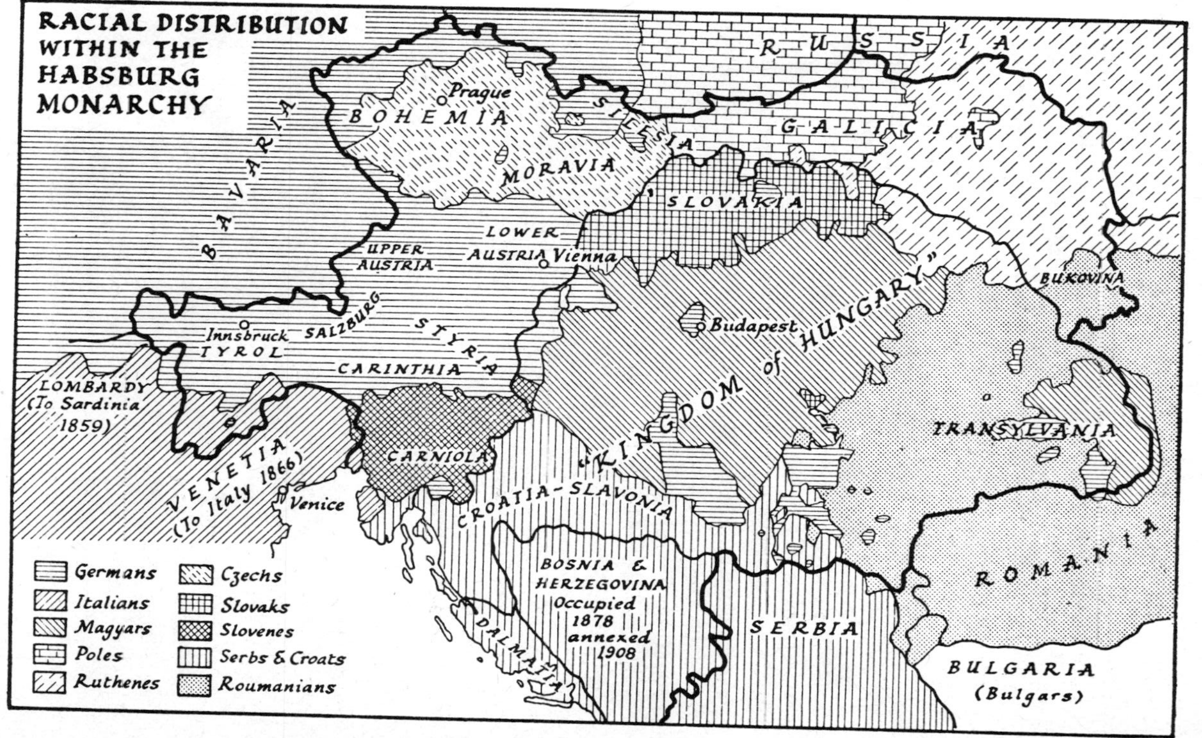
RACIAL DISTRIBUTION WITHIN THE HABSBURG MONARCHY
RUSSIA
BAVARIA
BOHEMIA
Prague
SILESIA
GALICIA
MORAVIA
SLOVAKIA
UPPER AUSTRIA
LOWER AUSTRIA
Vienna
BUKOVINA
SALZBURG
Innsbruck
TYROL
STYRIA
CARINTHIA
Budapest
"KINGDOM of HUNGARY"
LOMBARDY (To Sardinia 1859)
VENETIA (To Italy 1866)
Venice
CARNIOLA
TRANSYLVANIA
CROATIA-SLAVONIA
BOSNIA & HERZEGOVINA Occupied 1878 annexed 1908
SERBIA
ROMANIA
DALMATIA
BULGARIA (Bulgars)
Germans
Italians
Magyars
Poles
Ruthenes
Czechs
Slovaks
Slovenes
Serbs & Croats
Roumanians

even the Balkanization of the Balkans was preferable to their Ottomanization; and those who talk disparagingly of the Balkanization of eastern Europe might stop to consider that the only alternatives history has found for this region have been Germanization or Russification.

The real weakness of the Versailles system, however, lies not in the creation of the small states to the east and south of the Germans, but in the absence of any effective means of maintaining and defending their existence. For it is something of a dream-Europe with which the eye is confronted when it contemplates the political map in 1920; and it is a dream obviously dreamed by a backward-looking Frenchman. The Habsburgs, the more venerable of the enemies of the French, are destroyed altogether, and Germany, the newer enemy, is disarmed. Over against it is the client-state system of the great days of the *ancien régime*, only slightly modified. Poland is back again; that Poland whose partition was as much a symbol of the tragedy of the Bourbons as the fall of the Bastille itself. The friendly Ottoman Turk is gone, but in his place are his much more amenable heirs, Jugoslavia and Roumania, ready like him to contain or to harass the Germans; and if there was now no Bavaria to keep watch and ward on the French behalf, Czechoslovakia would fulfil the same function rather better. By 1927 France had alliances with all these states; but formal alliances were hardly necessary to underline the fact that the Versailles Settlement was almost (save for the unfortunate absence of a French client-state on the Rhine) a Frenchman's ideal Europe.

What made the map look even more old fashioned, all the more of a revival of the days of Louis XIV, was the fact that it showed Russia as almost completely excluded from Europe. This too was to the advantage of French diplomacy, if it could be maintained. Alliance with Russia had always carried with it the danger of subordinating French interests to

Russian; and it had been accepted at all only because the more sympathetic Poles had disappeared. Now in 1920 with Poland to look to in the east instead of the incalculable Russians, France was immeasurably more the master. Poland, for instance, could never involve France with England or Japan, as Russia might do.

It is not without justification therefore that the settlement was described by some critics as 'Clemenceau's peace' for no map of Europe save that drawn by Napoleon I had ever been more clearly marked 'made in France'. If ever a nation succeeded, France appeared to have succeeded by 1920 in the calculation she had made after Fashoda that it was in Europe and not in Africa that lay her best chances of national revival.

Unfortunately the dominating position which France now appeared to occupy in Europe was not the achievement of her own unaided skill and resolution as had been her achievements in the remote Bourbon past. The state system of Europe in 1920, apparently dedicated to a French hegemony, existed thanks to the superior resources and manpower of the British Empire and the United States; it existed also because Lenin and Trotsky had caused Russia to turn her back on Europe at Brest-Litovsk. In resources and manpower, France, when Versailles was really the capital of Europe and not merely the title of a peace treaty, had been the largest civilized state in the western world. Now she was not. The gravest weakness of the Versailles Settlement is therefore that it created a state system which depended exclusively on France to maintain it; for France was not strong enough.

The solution was to follow precedent and maintain in peace the coalition that had won the war; but the military guarantees for France which would alone have made a reality of the Versailles system were not forthcoming from either England or the United States. The consequence was that France was committed to that neurotic search for 'security' in

EUROPE
in
1914
UNITED KINGDOM
Scotland
Ireland
England
NORWAY
SWEDEN
DENMARK
HOLLAND
BELGIUM
LUX.
prussia
GERMAN EMPIRE
Rhine
Oder
Vistula
RUSSIA
Dnieper
Dniester
AUSTRIA-HUNGARY
FRANCE
SWITZ.
ITALY
Bosnia
MONTE-NEGRO
SERBIA
ALBANIA
RUMANIA
Danube
BULGARIA
GREECE
BLACK SEA
OTTOMAN EMPIRE
SPAIN
PORTUGAL
Corsica (Fr.)
Sardinia (It.)
Malta (Br.)
Cyprus (Br.)

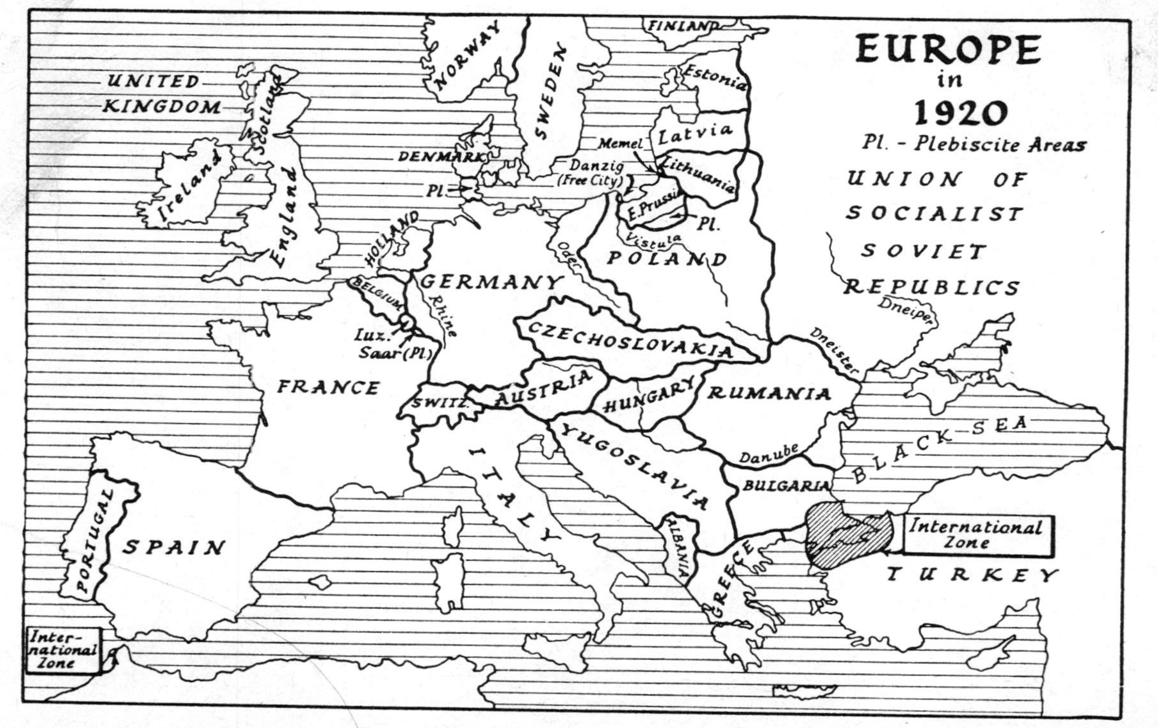
EUROPE
in
1920
Pl. - Plebiscite Areas
UNION OF
SOCIALIST
SOVIET
REPUBLICS
UNITED
KINGDOM
Scotland
Ireland
England
NORWAY
SWEDEN
FINLAND
Estonia
Latvia
Lithuania
Memel
Danzig
(Free City)
E. Prussia
Pl.
Vistula
POLAND
DENMARK
Pl.
HOLLAND
BELGIUM
Lux.
Saar (Pl.)
GERMANY
Oder
Rhine
CZECHOSLOVAKIA
FRANCE
SWITZ.
AUSTRIA
HUNGARY
RUMANIA
Dneiper
Dneister
Danube
BLACK SEA
BULGARIA
YUGOSLAVIA
ALBANIA
GREECE
ITALY
SPAIN
PORTUGAL
International
Zone
TURKEY
Inter-
national
Zone

the 1920's which so irritated her friends but was an inevitable consequence of the fact that the peace treaties imposed on France duties that were too great for her.

For England, France was, by 1919, what she had been in 1856—the loyal ally who had done too well out of the war. The general tendencies of British policy were made clear in Lloyd George's statements of March 1919:

> 'I would put in the forefront of the peace that once [Germany] accepts our terms, especially reparations, we . . . will do everything possible to enable the German people to get on their legs again. We cannot both cripple her and expect her to pay.'

This shows that England would henceforth see Germany as a balance in Europe against France; and it was also a British calculation that too rigorous a policy towards Germany would throw her into the arms of Russia. At the same time, Lloyd George revealed thus early a state of mind about Germany which found its fullest expression in the policy of Neville Chamberlain in 1938:

> 'I cannot conceive any greater cause of future war than that the German people . . . should be surrounded by a number of small states many of them consisting of people who have never previously set up a stable government for themselves but each of them containing large masses of Germans clamouring for reunion with their native land.'

This curious utterance reveals a strange lack of confidence in a settlement to which the British were themselves a party, and it expresses the German case against the Slavs in terms that anticipated those of Hitler. It reveals that, as the peace conference ended, the British had resumed that unawareness of realities which had characterized them in 1914. They had reverted to their former belief in the innate superiority of Germans over Frenchmen and Slavs. And it was sheer distortion to speak of the failure of the Slavs to set up stable governments 'for themselves'; it was as if the fact of ancient conquest automatically disqualified them from being liberated. One might also note Smuts' observation earlier to the effect that 'the people left behind by the decomposition of Russia, Austria and Turkey are mostly untried politically'. The truth was that the British did not much like the principle of self-determination. Although an acceptable slogan for encouraging the dissolution of the enemy from within, and for justifying the war to those many Americans still susceptible to phrases about '*entente* imperialism' it was a very dangerous slogan to the ears of an Imperial War Cabinet in London. Refusals to grant self-determination to Ireland, to India, to Egypt and to the Boers either had been or were about to be major issues in British politics. Once established as the sole principle of political justice it could mean the division of the empire into a series of independent sovereignties.

Yet what was really wrong with the principle was not that it was applied to the Slavs in 1919, but that the Germans, in Germany and out of it, applied it to themselves from 1932 onwards. Its application to the Slavs was in fact the sole guarantee of peace; and it was not in the direction of Prague or Warsaw that British warnings should have been sent, but to Berlin. Of course, considered without reference to circumstances, the principle of self-determination is destructive of peace and of morality; but the only people in Europe who were in a position to produce war, and the subjugation of others if they attempted to apply it recklessly, were the Germans. In losing sight of this fact and leaving the French and the Slavs to cope with the Germans unaided, the British committed a cardinal error not unlike the error of neutralism they all but committed in 1914.

It is thus not true that the east European states provided an inadequate bulwark against Germany. They were a quite adequate device for preventing that German domination of the non-Germans which had for so long been the characteristic feature of east European history. Nor is it a fair criticism of the settlement to say that these states were a temptation to the Germans to make a war. It was not their weakness but that of the wartime allies that proved the real incitement to the Germans. Equally irrelevant is the argument that their existence was in some way artificial because it depended on the weakness of Russia after 1917. There is much to be said for the view that it was a strong Russia rather than a weak Russia that better served their security. Certainly, while Germany was the only potential threat to them, a strong Russia was as necessary a guarantee of their safety as a strong France backed by Great Britain and the United States.

At this point it is relevant to notice how much harm was done by the setting up of the League of Nations in 1919. The peace could be preserved only by the great powers who had so arduously earned it. Only an alliance of Great Britain, the United States, France and Russia to defend the treaties by force of arms could keep Germany within bounds, as the facts eventually proved. But the first three powers were afraid of Bolshevism, and were themselves regarded by the Russians as nothing more than imperialist interventionists; the United States wanted to go on pretending that Europe did not exist; the British wanted German markets for their goods, and resented the power and the ruthlessness of the French. A League of Nations which excluded Germany, from which the United States and Russia excluded themselves, and in which the British pursued one policy and the French an entirely different one, had the disastrous effect of presenting a war-weary public opinion with the mere shadow of collective security. Worse still, it was a shadow just substantial enough to prevent people from realizing that an effective peace-preserving machinery was simply not there. Even if the machinery had been there, raucous voices would still have been raised in condemnation of it as 'Great Power domination' or as 'return to the balance of power'. In a famous, but coolly-received phrase, Neville Chamberlain was later to say that it was 'midsummer madness' to suppose that the League of Nations could protect anyone from aggression. Unfortunately the words had been true from the day of the League's foundation. No lesson was writ larger over the history of the nineteenth century than the simple one that just as only great powers could start wars, only the great powers could prevent them. The League of Nations was a failure because that lesson was ignored.

INDEX